Supporting Early Language Development

Early years practitioners, parents and carers, childminders, health visitors, do you need effective ideas for giving your babies and toddlers support to become confident talkers?

National research shows that poor language and communication skills have a profound effect on the life chances of children and young people. This highly practical book will enable you to give children in your care the help they need to build their crucial language skills at the earliest point in their development.

Based on the author's highly regarded SPIRALS language development programme, the book provides over 40 tried and tested sessions to help develop children's early speech, language and communication. Each language concept is introduced one at a time and builds on the most frequently used words by infants. It suggests ways to use music, repetition, simple meaningful gestures and signing to reinforce children's understanding.

Features include:

- clear guidelines for introducing specific games and activities at the right developmental level for babies and toddlers to develop their language skills from 0 to $3^{1}/_{2}$ years;
- ideas for progression based on child development;
- insights into the underlying psychology of the activities we suggest;
- advice on when to begin to use small-group activities;
- guidance on what to do if a child is reluctant to join in;
- practical suggestions for involving parents as partners;
- photocopiable recording sheets;
- suggestions for further reading and resources.

Written by a leading authority in the field, this exciting new resource provides everything you need to support young children's language skills at the earliest point in their development.

Marion Nash is a Chartered Educational Psychologist with 24 years' experience and a specialist interest in early speech, language and communication. Since 2002 Marion has provided SPIRALS language training for early years settings, primary schools, speech and language therapy service teams and local authorities. The course is also offered via 'I Can', the national speech and language charity.

Jackie Lowe is a Highly Specialist Speech and Language Therapist currently working with the 'I Can' Nursery Centre in Plymouth, supporting children with specific language impairments.

David Leah is a Consultant in Further Education at Spirals Training.

Together they have produced this effective guidance for everyone working with babies and toddlers, which is easy to use and will be a helpful resource in your busy day.

Supporting Early Language Development

SPIRALS for babies and toddlers

Marion Nash
with Jackie Lowe and David Leah

Routledge
Taylor & Francis Group

LONDON AND NEW YORK

First published 2013
by Routledge
2 Park Square, Milton Park, Abingdon, Oxon OX14 4RN

Simultaneously published in the USA and Canada
by Routledge
711 Third Avenue, New York, NY 10017

Routledge is an imprint of the Taylor & Francis Group, an informa business

British Library Cataloguing in Publication Data
A catalogue record for this book is available from the British Library

Library of Congress Cataloging in Publication Data
Supporting early language development : spirals for babies and toddlers /
Marion Nash, Jackie Lowe, David Leah.
p. cm.
ISBN 978-0-415-69756-9 (pbk.) – ISBN 978-0-203-13874-8 (e-book)
1. Children–Language. 2. Language arts (Early childhood) I. Lowe, Jackie.
II. Leah, David. III. Title.
LB1139.L3N295 2012
372.6–dc23
2012008208

ISBN: 978-0-415-69756-9 (pbk)
ISBN: 978-0-203-13874-8 (ebk)

Typeset in Helvetica and Garamond
by FiSH Books, Ltd, Enfield

Printed and bound in Great Britain by the MPG Books Group

Contents

To Tom, Dan, Keri, Emily, Leah, Geo, Neela and their wonderful parents. To Holly, George and Doodle. Also, to all those caring people everywhere who support young children in developing their language and communication skills.

List of contributors

I would like to thank everyone who has been so positive about the idea of a *Baby Spirals* resource. Special thanks are due to our family and friends who have encouraged us along the way. Thanks are due to the Harlow and Oxford children's centres and nurseries who trialled the very early versions of *Baby Spirals* and to Laura Halstead and Anthea Williams in Oxford for their research into the positive impact of *Spirals* on young children's language. Thanks, too, in Plymouth, to Meryl Wilson, Nicky Walters, Kate Gillett and Mel O'Leary of our Early Years Advisory Service for their time and preview of *Baby Spirals* and their helpful suggestions. Also to I Can, the national charity that supports children's speech language and communication, and to Kassia Morris in Cardiff; they have both provided access to *Spirals* training for many practitioners and made a difference to so many children. My appreciation also goes to Annie and Lesley for their wise words. Thanks are also due to Jean Gross, CBE for her professional guidance and advice and her championing of children's roles as little scientists exploring the world.

Foreword

Good communication and language skills are vital for children's life chances. We now know that vocabulary at age 5 is one of the best predictors of how many GCSEs a child will get when they are 16, and the best predictor of all of whether a child brought up in poverty will escape poverty as an adult.

Conversely, we know that poor language skills can lead to long-term problems. 65 per cent of young offenders, for example, have been found to have significant speech, language and communication difficulties – in most cases never known about until they got into trouble.

So language really matters...and the foundations of good language and communication are laid before a child is 3. By this time 80 per cent of children's brain development is complete. Eighteen months is the peak 'window of opportunity' for language learning. School readiness at 5 is already determined by whether a child has a good vocabulary and speaks in two–three-word sentences at the age of 2.

In my two years as the government's Communication Champion for Children, I became ever more convinced that we have to put more emphasis on getting language right before children are 3, rather than just wait until they are older. This means that the baby room is the most important place in the setting. And with many more disadvantaged two-year-olds due to receive government funding for 15 hours of free early education, it will be essential that practitioners working with this age group get support in how best to foster children's communication development.

This book provides that support. As a long-time fan of the *Spirals* language development materials for older children, I was delighted to know that materials for under-3s would be available. I think the ideas, like the face-to-face games, vocabulary baskets and concept baskets, are brilliant – really fun and do-able. There is a great blend of child-initiated and adult-led learning, good links to the new Early Years Foundation Stage framework, and ideas on how settings can share what they are doing with parents.

I know practitioners will want to grab the book and get going with it straight away. I'm looking forward to my next grandchild so that I can try the ideas out too!

Jean Gross CBE
Communication Champion for Children, 2009–11

Introduction

Children begin to develop language from birth, and their progress depends on warm and positive interaction in safe, stimulating environments. A flow of conversation that is responsive to a child's interests and abilities is essential to their language and wider development. Children need opportunities to move and to explore their surroundings through all their senses, to talk with adults and to play with them. Without this a child's development is likely to suffer, limiting their capacity to engage with new people and situations, and to learn new skills.

(Dame Clare Tickell, 2011)[1]

Section 1 contains important training guidance on working with early language development and gives guidance on how to make the best of the ideas in this *Spirals* book. The guidance in the first part of the book forms a training component that links really well to early years staff development.

In Section 2 we outline games and activities that develop key language and communication skills. We cannot cover all the language children will need, but this section will give you ideas as to how to go about developing effective support systems for language in your home or setting. Once young children are keyed into learning language with you through these and similar activities, they really will be in an upward spiral of learning.

Marion and Jackie have written a series of practical books. *Spirals Language Development* is aimed at supporting practitioners and parents to develop the language communication and thinking skills of four- to eight-year-old children. The feedback for them nationally has been tremendously positive. Now, due to demand, they have got together again to develop a book for practitioners and parents working and living with babies and toddlers. The activities can be easily blended into the day and work well with other super language and communication initiatives that also look to establish and promote language learning-friendly environments. This book is based on 24 years' practice for Marion as an educational psychologist with an early years and language specialism, and 23 years for Jackie as a speech and language therapist. They have authored six books in the *Spirals* series for schools and early years settings and parents to support effective language development. David Leah has been part of senior management in an FE college and is now an educational consultant and an experienced verifier and moderator for qualifications including NVQs at a national level.

Essentially, this book shows how and when to introduce powerful but simple activities and games to support the children's progress in language and communication, which will stand them in good stead in preparing them for life and particularly when entering school. The ideas incorporate up-to-date research in brain-based learning and psychology. They include opportunities for child-led exploration and adult scaffolding of learning. We bring to mind key areas throughout the book in ways that we hope will be easy to remember in your busy day.

Note

1. Tickell, C. (2011) *The Early Years Foundations for Life, Health and Learning.* An independent report on the Early Years Foundation Stage to Her Majesty's Government.

Section 1

More about this book

One day when I was running a 'welcome to nursery' session, I met a lovely mum who was absolutely aware of the best food to give her lovely twin babies and the best way to care for them practically. Then I started talking to the group about the need to talk to babies from the earliest moment so that they can build their early language skills. This lovely mum shocked me by saying, with a laugh, that she never talked to her babies, as they couldn't answer her and she would feel silly speaking to them. I never forgot that day and this book is perhaps the result. Of course, we *must* speak to babies as soon as they are born, even before! Adults are so important in mediating the environment, making it more understandable for them, so that babies and young children can learn about language and life.

In this book Jackie and I are building on what we do in our work. We want passionately to remind everyone who spends time with babies and toddlers how important they are to the children they care for. We want to keep repeating the message that you need to give quality face-to-face time talking and communicating with the child from birth (or before) as well as supporting the child to investigate the world for themselves through exploration and play as little  scientists and explorers. This book will give you practical ideas, based in psychology, on how to provide vital language and communication skills with your babies and toddlers using play activities that you are both likely to enjoy.

This book is aimed at supporting the practice of practitioners working with babies and the younger preschool child up to three-and-a-half years of age. David looked at the first section of the book as a training guide for personal and professional development for practitioners. It would also be particularly useful for parents, carers, health visitors and childminders.

The first section of the book is intended to be used for everyday guidance in supporting language and communication development with the children. Practitioners in early years settings supporting older children with moderate-to-significant language delay will also find the guidance useful using the developmental sequence of the language rather than the age levels. The nature of the delay would guide the practitioner as to the best developmental level to which gear the activities and games for the child.

Language develops in a sequence in a spiral process and we can use many activities and strategies to support this. Each child will need different-sized steps in the spiral of learning; some children will cope well with bigger jumps while others will need tiny steps and lots of repetition and reinforcement to help them remember and use what they have learned. For young children we want to provide contexts that will foster play that will naturally elicit certain types of language and repeat the key language for the child. The traditional treasure baskets and vocabulary treasure baskets can be used to provide lots of lovely opportunities for babies to practise exploring everyday objects. These can be exciting for the young child.

Next, at nine months, we suggest the introduction of vocabulary baskets to help to develop naming of objects through play. The concept treasure baskets come next in the spiral of language learning; they give the child the chance to explore objects that are big and little and to begin to understand the meaning of the concept words. They learn about what happens when we say 'more'. They also need the chance to learn about 'more' in different contexts such as at snack, when they are offered more drink, or in the sand tray when you ask if they would like more sand in their bucket, or more water in their jug in the water play area. This makes a bridge of learning and experience from your activities to other areas of the child's experience. Its not that we don't say these words to children but that we need to make sure that we all do it consistently and often enough for it to make a difference their language

Older infants can explore a 'verb box' with objects that help them to explore particular action words with you; so, for example, they may find various objects to interact with actively, such as a brush, and then they can hear and use the words 'brush' and 'brushing' in their play. We cannot include all the necessary words and concepts and skill developments in this book but we have included key examples, and these should give ideas for further activities that practitioners and parents can develop in order to continue their good work.

Signing and meaningful gestures are highly recommended to help children's understanding and use of communication. However, please note that just as we should not overload a child with spoken language, we also should not overload them with signing or gesture. Choose signs to support the key word or concept you are working on. Give parents a little guide so that they can use and understand the children's signs at home too.

A friend who has worked with mothers and their babies and toddlers for many years asked me to say that signing *supports* talking; it goes alongside it. She was concerned that sometimes people tend to use signs instead of talking to their baby. You need to use the sign to support the key word as you are saying it.

An important message for practitioners, parents, older brothers and sisters, grandparents, childminders

You all have such an important part to play in helping babies and toddlers to be successful in reaching the highest spiral of learning that they can. Developing a child's language will support them in developing their other important areas of learning and give them valuable life skills.

Practitioners can choose activities to be sent home to parents to give them new ideas for ways to promote language opportunities with their children. Then the equipment and ideas are all ready to hand for parents to use at home with their child. A camera could be sent home for parents to take photographs of the child involved in the activities, and this could be included to record a child's learning journey. A simple explanation of each activity is all that is needed as the games and ideas are self-explanatory. There are suggestions in this book for what you can do if you find that a child cannot play a particular game or won't join in an activity with you.

Every child is an individual and will have their own pace of learning. Some children have a brisk pace while others need more time for thinking things through, and we need to respect this.

Marion provides flexible training courses at different levels. These can be seen on her website (www.spiralstraining.co.uk). There is also an outline of training courses available at the back of this book. David is an FE specialist and can advise on queries regarding training.

Four learning spirals explained

Spiral of language learning

Young babies and toddlers are developing the key skills that underpin their later language learning. These skills involve looking, focusing listening, attending and concentrating for longer and longer periods. Long before a baby can speak, they begin to develop an understanding of how communication works. They need to build their store of knowledge in their early years to support their progress in all areas of talk. Understanding can be supported through gesture and signing. Spoken language begins with sounds. Babies begin to experiment with sounds and we call that babbling. Words begin to emerge and a growing vocabulary that the child can understand and then learn to speak. Concepts are more difficult to grasp and need to be experienced with concrete examples that they can watch alongside the words that describe them. Examples of early concepts are *on, off, more, in, out, big, little*, whereas the concept of *under* comes later. Language is then developed further by the older child into longer phrases and early sentences. If babies are 'saturated' with the experience of hearing language, as long as they don't have any specific difficulties they can learn the names for things and then concepts, and then come to understand and use them. These are the spirals of language learning that we support in this book.

Spiral of learning about communication

Babies need help to learn how to act with other people. You can help this development by lots of face-to-face activities using gestures, sing-song rhymes and facial expressions to show how turn-taking in communicating with others works and how to recognise and express emotions. The young child needs to learn that communication is a two-way process. At first this will be within the immediate family. The young child will soon need to know how to act with people outside the immediate family, practitioners in their early years setting, other children, teachers, teaching and mealtime assistants, and people they meet in the community. They need to learn to understand the feelings and actions of others in order to become skilled communicators. Learning to say 'please' and 'thank you' and to take turns is all very important to help the child to develop good social skills and understanding of other people's needs. Children also need a grasp of the meaning of body language as well as talk. That is why one-to-one, focused sessions with a key adult are so important.

Spiral of experiential learning

Most children learn best by experiencing a concept physically. Babies and toddlers can be supported through *Spirals* activities to learn by experiencing language-related concepts through touch, sound and sight. This supports the development of memory and recall. Next, when the child is ready to use their knowledge from that personal experience, you can support them with a new *Spiral* level of activities. For example, with the concept *on*, the child will play games that show some different ways the word 'on' can be used, for example as in putting clothes *on*, or jumping *on* a mat. The *Spirals* activities are provided to help the input necessary for the child to name and then to understand the meanings of words, and later on when they are developmentally ready they can be encouraged to *use* the word themselves as output. This is the spiral of learning consolidated through experience.

Spiral of confidence

Babies process and communicate their thoughts and feelings from birth. When babies and toddlers see adults smiling at them and experience enjoyable activities with them using simple words, rhymes and songs, it has a positive effect on their image of talk and of themselves as a person. When they can begin to predict when an activity is about to begin and end it helps to develop confidence and trust in the process. This can spiral as the child learns that the adult is interested in following their lead and respect their point of view as they explore the world. Children begin experimenting with more words and longer phrases. They become confident that they have a voice worth listening to and this leads them to be more confident communicators as they connect communicating with positive emotions. You can help children to love language and interacting through talk and song and this can begin to include sharing some lovely books. This is all a powerful support for the child's emotional, linguistic and social development throughout life.

Training guidance

Very important guidance: please read this *before going on to the activities.*

We need to promote and cherish the children's own exploration and interests and to keep them safe as they explore the world. Adult-led language activities are very important but these should be only part of the day's language activities and used sensitively. They should be enjoyable and short, one minute at a time for babies, repeated up to five times a day in the setting and with parents and carers.

Promote child-initiated learning

This book presents ideas for adult-led activities that are very important in providing language input that the children can use to make progress in their understanding of the way communication and language work. However, we must be very clear that these adult-led sessions are brief and are to be embedded in a much wider context of child-initiated learning within the setting.

Children, even the very youngest, need clear routines and sensible boundaries, but within this, our guidance for children in the Early Years Foundation Stage makes it clear that our youngest children have a need for a high proportion of their learning to be self-initiated. They need to be little explorers and scientists, finding out about their environment and how it works. It is so important to develop a child's interest in learning. This is what will carry them through those difficult moments in life when learning something is a bit hard. They will not just give up on it but will use that interest to keep them trying to solve the puzzles life presents them with. You will also have given them lots of strategies to try when solving puzzles in the little games you play with them now.

How to help children to get the best out of the activities

Is the child ready to take part?

Remember to choose your moments when the child is alert and wants to play. Let them know when activities are about to change and respect them by taking their mood into account. It will affect their readiness to learn from you.

Help children to achieve at their individual level

Children should not be expected to achieve activities beyond their developmental level, although, of course, children may surprise you! But they can play games at a level they are comfortable with, which will develop a range of skills that will help their learning. Within that, you can extend the child's skills a little at a time. The activities in this book develop children's skills in very small stages to provide small but consistent progress in the learning spirals of the child. In this way learning is fun. Some children will be able to make bigger leaps in their learning, but we need to make sure that learning is secure. The beauty of using games is that children are happy to play again and again so reinforcement is built into the process.

Progress is not always straightforward

 Children are all individuals and will reach milestones at different times when they are ready developmentally. Sometimes a child will appear to stop progressing in one area, but that can be because energy for learning is being diverted to some other skill. Sometimes there will be a leap forward when least expected. This is where your observation and checking is really important.

Problem-solving

If a child doesn't join in your games

It is always worth trying a little game or song to distract a fretful baby or toddler but you may then discover that they need a hug instead, or a short nap. If you are concerned because a child continues to decline to interact with you, it is sensible to raise your concerns in the setting. If a child continues not to join in, there can be several reasons for this, so the main thing to do is to work out the reasons why the child isn't joining in the games.

Could it be lack of confidence?

Explore to see if the child is unsure or lacking in self-confidence. If so, let them observe you playing the games with another child. If the child is very inattentive, ask if another adult can sit them on their lap and encourage them to watch you playing the game with another child in order to get an idea of what will be expected. Another idea is to ask another adult to join you for the couple of minutes the game lasts, holding the child and supporting them to play the game with you. You could also ask parents if they could try playing the game at home when the child is relaxed and see if the child can enter into it with them. This will give an opportunity to play it in the setting after practising it. Could mum or dad come in one session and play it with their child?

Is it over-excitement?

Sometimes children can be over-excited and may see efforts to involve them in a focused game as an opportunity for playing chase! If this is a regular response, try to choose a time when the child is calmer and make the game interesting by your tone of voice, raising their curiosity by commenting, 'Oooh, what is this? Uh oh, what do I do?' Or try singing in a sing-song rhyme about playing the game. Singing a little song can alert children that you are going to play a game with them and can help them to focus their attention more quickly as they look forward to the activities. Then see if they respond. If not, try entering little play situations that they have created themselves to signal mutual interest and respect and see if this encourages them to join in with your games. You might be able to let them take a small toy from their play as a little bridge when they come to play your game.

Is the child distracted?

Make sure the child isn't distracted by interesting items nearby or a colourful display just behind you when you have your focused time. Have a neutral screen or wall behind you. A colleague, Nicky, told me about her 'Nicky's magic red cloth', which is now used in nurseries all over the place. Red is for *stop* accompanied by a raised-hand gesture. The cloth goes over any tabletop activities; for example, instruments on the music table that are to be used later but are distracting for a child in a focused task. Children learn not to touch unless there is an adult with them. But they will be allowed to see or play with the things later. Children soon learn to respond well to this as they see the meaning as clear and fair.

Is the child unaware?

Sometimes children can be unaware of activities about to happen. You can sew little bells into feely bags to attract attention and take the play objects out of these feely bags, so children can explore by touch as well as sight.

Is the activity at the right developmental age for the child?

Developmental norms are provided in a simple chart. However, it is so important to start at the level each child is comfortable with and gently extend the level. Children achieve at different levels and also will progress differently in different areas. Some children are very skilled physically but less forward in their language. Some children will have ability but will not be able to show it due to shyness and lack of confidence. Some children will show delays in their skill areas. You may find that with practice and experience the child begins to move ahead, though maybe not quickly.

Could the child be anxious or stressed?

If a child is stressed, the part of the brain that registers emotion is triggered before the thinking, rational brain, and if the signals are too strong, the brain goes into freeze or flight mode for survival, and learning is blocked. Memory is blocked. Try taking the child for a little walk in the outside play area before the activity. Allow them to observe other children playing the games with you so that they can see they are relaxing and fun. Try at first having the focused time in one of the little semi-enclosed spaces like a communication-friendly 'tent' or playhouse where it is quiet and where the child's startle response won't be triggered by any noises nearby.

What to do if you are concerned?

If a child is not showing signs of progress and continues not to interact with you, what is the best thing to do? If you become concerned about a child's developmental progress, it is good practice to raise these concerns with the member of staff in your setting who is responsible for deciding whether a child has an additional need for support. In England, for example, this would be the special needs co-ordinator (SENCo). Every local authority has different ways of requesting support from their early years advisory service if needed. Parents need to be consulted at the start of any concerns you may have. If you are a parent or carer who has concerns about your child's progress, then approach your health visitor and discuss your concerns with your child's key worker in their setting.

Using this book

Timing

In the language-minute sessions the adult is leading the play and exploration with the child and strengthening their grasp of language. Over the rest of the day adults should be looking for naturally occurring opportunities to comment on what the child is doing and to give them the words for what is going on around them. This narrative, or story about what is going on in the day, is also very important for children to hear. They will begin to pick out words and phrases you use often. With the support of the adult-led sessions children have a base on which to build their understanding and to begin to say the words themselves with meaning.

How much time to spend on focused talk

Babies and toddlers are full of energy and want to explore the world on their own terms, so don't be surprised if it takes a little while for them to understand and join in the games or if they can't focus for very long.

For *babies*, we suggest one-minute language focus with an adult-led activity.

For children of two years and above, you will be able to judge if you can engage them comfortably in a longer session of three to five minutes of face-to-face, focused language play with an adult, or if they need a shorter session. It should be geared to the individual need of each child. We would recommend one or two of these longer, focused language sessions each day and one of these can be at home. When parents and practitioners work on language activities together they provide a bedrock of support that gives the child the best chance in life.

Please remember that when we talk about adult-led sessions we are only talking about part of the talk the child needs to experience in a day. They need to hear adults talking simply about what is going on around them as part of the language background.

Children also need to hear praise and genuine comments about their attempts and successes, whether big or little.

Keep parents involved as key partners who also have the child's interests at heart. Children thrive when they hear positive messages about themselves from their families.

Working with parents and in the setting

Once you have had the chance to see how some of the games and activities work, you might think of inviting parents in for a little baby language circle. In the circle together you could observe babies and respond to their sounds and actions and also look at how to involve the babies in activity songs like 'Row Your Boat', 'Hickory Dickory Dock' or 'The Grand Old Duke of York', and ask parents for ideas too. You could share with parents how treasure baskets work in your setting and give ideas that could be used at home to fill home baskets. You could include vocabulary baskets and concept-basket sessions for the parents of children who are at that stage of development. The contents list and guidance in this book should be helpful.

Safety is of course a main concern when deciding what toys and material to provide for the activities. Look at the materials carefully and make sure they have no small pieces or sharp edges. Also be aware that young children will want to explore things with their mouth and chew them, so check for safety. Never use balloons as toys. Wooden toys should be checked regularly for any splinters or rough surfaces. Items that are made of small pieces, such as a string of beads, should be tested often to make sure they will not come apart. Long strings and scarves etc. should not be included for young children. Baskets and containers should be shallow and within the reach of the child. Treasure-basket play of any sort must always be carefully supervised to ensure the child explores safely.

By careful risk assessment, preparation of the materials and the environment, and close observation of the young child at play, you can prepare the way for the child to enjoy and take what they need from the activities. They can relax, follow their interests and explore their environment in fun ways as well as interacting with you through play. Making use of the suggested activities in this book at the right developmental stage for each child and embedding them in child-initiated exploration will enhance the child's language and communication alongside their cognitive and emotional growth in a healthy way.

Training guidance

Language input is presented in three key ways over the child's day

1. *Follow the child's lead but give them words for what they are doing (commenting on children's self-initiated play)*

As Dame Clare Tickell says:

> A flow of conversation that is responsive to a child's interests and abilities is essential to their language and wider development.[1]

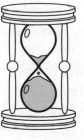

Young children benefit from hearing adults talk about what is happening around them. This 'narrative' usually repeats many key words, concepts and phrases in a familiar context. This should be the largest part of the language input in any day. Also, at times during the day, we can make time to observe babies and toddlers and watch carefully to see what their focus of interest is. When it seems natural we can comment on what a child is doing in their play using a child's name. First let them know that we are talking about something to do with them and give them some key words for their activity. Comment without interrupting their flow of action. Keep your words to a minimum. Be content to use long pauses between your comments. Babies and toddlers can only understand very small chunks of talk at any one time. Some children have the ability to tip in and out of the adult language around them; others do not yet have the level of skill they need to do this successfully. Until it becomes clear which situation a child is in, you don't want to overload the child with talk; it is best to use the same simple phrase several times in a session rather than keep introducing new ones. That way the child will link the words with meaning. Use the same words for an activity each time. For example, 'Lily's painting.' 'Aled's building.' 'Patrick's looking.' You can also sometimes make these into little friendly tunes like a little song.

2. Face-to-face language minutes (focused, talk-based activity for one to five minutes with an adult)

Interactive time. Engage children so that they can touch, feel, see and hear the activities with you. With babies and toddlers, lift them to your eye level or bring your face close to the child's so that they can see and focus on your expressions. Exaggerate your expressions and gestures a little to attract and keep the child's attention. Adjust the support you give to the child's age and ability. For example, just roll a soft ball to the baby, then roll it back yourself while singing a little song with key words in it. An increasingly mobile child can take a more active part. Carry little ones around so they experience the world in a different way, hear your comments on it and see your pleasure in their responses. The adult can shape the language through the materials they use. The main thing is to use materials that are safe and attractive for the child. Also use your voice as a musical/rhythmical instrument and your face to model and share feelings. Use gesture and some signing, and, very importantly, relax and have fun. Fun and joy have a positive effect on the ability of the brain to remember and retrieve information; so enjoying time with you will help babies and children to learn.

3. Building on language-minute play (providing opportunities that can be used to reinforce key language through extended play and exploration)

We need to spend some time each day building on the key language provided in the adult-led session. This should be part of following the flow of child-initiated activities and modelling essential language skills over the day. But for this short time the language you focus on is guided by the content of the language minutes for the day. The adult follows the toddler's activities, with an eye on safety, showing interest in what the toddler is engaging with and providing a repetition of the simple language from the five-minute focus session. So, for example, if you have been working on the concept word 'on', you could observe the child in play, both inside and outside, and play and talk simply about the child being *on* the mat, *on* the slide or *on* the bicycle. If there is time, you could repeat the same language minutes that day to really reinforce the language.

Minimise distractions

Note

1. Tickell, C. (2011) *The Early Years Foundations for Life, Health and Learning.* An independent report on the Early Years Foundation Stage to Her Majesty's Government.

Suggested four-step plan for each day

Think of providing language input through the day as if you are mixing liquid chocolate with cream in a glass. As you begin to stir the two together there is a wide band of chocolate, and a few minutes later it becomes a narrow strip, then gets broader again. It keeps changing as you work on it. It goes with the flow but is always there to be seen. The two liquids tip into and out of each other and swirl and blend. Sometimes you see more chocolate, sometimes you see more cream and sometimes the two blend so well that you see a completely new colour. (*Note from Jackie*: Marion often talks about chocolate in her training too!)

During the day, blend your language inputs with the child's interests, activities and routines. Be flexible and aware. Be happy to move from adult-led play to child-led play so that if a child initiates a different game in your focus time you can support them in their game and then look for other opportunities to reintroduce yours. This could be in the same session or later in the day or even the next day. This can make a lovely flow, with adult and child taking turns as you blend the time you both spend together. Sometimes the language play will be longer and more focused and at other times appear in the background of the child's experience. Sometimes it will go so well that the child will make a new direction in the game themselves and change it completely so that it becomes a new game.

Suggested plan for each day:

1. During the day, follow the child's flow and give words simply. Identify times when the child is engaged in an activity and give simple words for what they are doing without interrupting their exploration. Repeat key words. Avoid overloading the child with talk or too many signs.

2. For young babies, have at least five of the one-minute focused talk sessions during the day with an adult, and record (charts are included for you to use). For the older child, have *at least* one five-minute focused talk and play session. Choose your time and content for the session with respect for the learning readiness of the child. Remember that this time is not additional to the work you are already doing. With the babies, the minute can and, in many cases, should be done alongside other activities such as nappy changing and feeding; the same for the toddlers talking about what they are doing.

3. Follow a face-to-face focused session with a period of interactive play with the child, following their flow of exploration and activity in their surroundings, using the language you have been using in the focused session wherever you reasonably can. Parents and carers can continue this at home.

4. If appropriate, follow this with another focused session of face-to-face focused activity later in the day to reinforce the key language.

Six-stage spirals of language support to blend into each day

The main ingredient is child-initiated play

What can be really effective is a six-stage spiral of action where we find out which activities and key language a child needs and build on this information. Think of a spiral of action where you do the following:

 Observe – Plan – Do – Reinforce – Repeat – Check and record – Observe again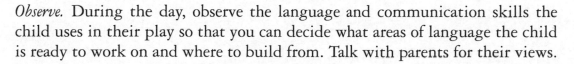

Observe. During the day, observe the language and communication skills the child uses in their play so that you can decide what areas of language the child is ready to work on and where to build from. Talk with parents for their views.

Plan. You can decide from your observations and information which key language and language activities to work on that day or that week. Also *plan* what tasks to ask parents to be involved in to support the child.

Do. Follow the child's activity flow and interests, and give words simply. Identify times when the child is engaged in an activity and give simple words for what they are doing without interrupting their exploration. Repeat key words. Avoid overloading the child with talk or too many signs. Also, run the planned language activities in short adult-led play sessions. For young babies, have at least five of the one-minute adult-led sessions during the day. Parents can join in these and add their minutes. For the older child of two years and over, have at least one, maybe two, three- to five-minute adult-led play sessions. Choose your time and content for the session with respect for the learning readiness of the child.

Reinforce. Provide other opportunities in practice. Follow each face-to-face adult-led session of play with a period of interactive play following the child's flow of exploration and activity, using the language you have been using in the focused session wherever you reasonably can. Follow play both indoors and outdoors where different activities take place. Parents and carers can continue this valuable input at home.

Repeat. If appropriate, follow this free play with another adult-led session on the same activity later in the day to reinforce key language. It is better to focus on one area of language over a week than to introduce too many areas and changes.

Check and record. Stand back and watch the child's own initiated play again to see if the child is absorbing and using the language. It may not be immediately apparent but look for small signs. You can decide whether the child is ready, developmentally, for this stage or needs an earlier one or maybe a later one. Make a note in the child's language record, which we have included (we have included a vocabulary check list further on).

Then, back to the first step to observe what the child needs next.

With young babies or children with motor difficulties, support them to join in physically with their environment as you comment on their *actions*.

Training guidance

Please, use rhyme and song and little musical jingles!

Music and movement develops language, memory and higher-level thinking.

Often essential language structures can be absorbed as part of learning a sequence of words in a song. Being able to keep a rhythmic beat is an important learning process. Studies have shown the importance of learning to keep a steady beat as this helps to feel the rhythm of language and actively involves the vestibular system that is involved in balance and movement, but also prepares the brain for learning. The many aspects of rhythm and music affect different parts of the brain. One side of the brain processes the words of a song while the other processes the music. When the whole brain is activated, memory is strengthened and the brain is prepared for working from both hemispheres. 'Keeping the beat' early activities can be used to help children acquire knowledge they will need later on when they begin to read. For example, children need to know that each word is spoken separately and can be represented by a written symbol, the written words they will see in books or in maths work. Musical activities also help the brain to process higher-level thinking. This is all very important as learning becomes more complex especially as the child enters formal schooling. Children who have had more practice in musical activities and keeping a steady beat are generally thought to be more prepared for the academic learning challenges, and this helps their confidence and self-esteem.

Also the combination of memories held in different parts of the brain come together and can be processed as one string of information using a song format. This is a tremendous support for retention of information. Think about it – many of the adverts we remember have songs attached to them. You didn't really try to learn the words; they just came with watching and hearing them with the music on a frequent basis.

Remembering made easy!

Maryann Harman, who writes on the important effects music and movement have on the brain, says this:

'When we put instruments in a child's hands in the early years, we are teaching them an activity that is positive and will last them a lifetime. What a wonderful gift to give our children!'[1]

These instruments can be, very simply, wooden spoons to bang on a tin, or a saucepan or a home-made shaker. We can also show children how to use their voice as an instrument to communicate emotions and messages. In *Spirals* activities we want to use our knowledge of this amazing human musical skill to our children's advantage and you are encouraged to use little jingles and songs in your interactions. We want to use rhyme and song and music and movement to support powerful learning of the key language skills and vocabulary children need to know. It is also important to know that when we move while we are learning, the brain processes the information in different ways. Young children especially need to move because they best understand concepts when they experience them through active play.[2] So moving to music and introducing rhyme to our activities is important, and in *Spirals* we emphasise this where we feel it could be introduced easily. Don't worry about feeling 'silly' or getting the words wrong if you are singing or making up a little rhyming song. This really will help the child. They won't mind if it's not perfect every time, they will just love your attention and be intrigued and interested by what you are doing; and after a while you will begin to relax and enjoy it as much as they do.

Notes

1. Maryann Harman, *Music and Movement for Early Childhood News – Instrumental in Language Development*. (http://musicwithmar.com)
2. Eric Jensen, *Teaching with the Brain in Mind: Books*, 2nd edn. ASCD Books, 2005. (http://www.earlychildhoodnews.com/earlychildhood/article_view.aspx?ArticleID=601)

Choose your time

Be guided by your child. What is your child's behaviour telling you?

Am I active and ready to engage?
Am I seeking your attention?

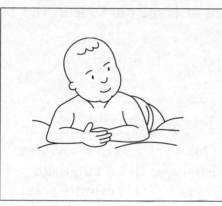

Am I in a listening mood?

Am I sleepy and needing to rest?

Am I distressed? What do I need?
Comfort? Distraction? Food or a drink?

Ideas to ensure continuity: recording

Five language minutes a day stars for the baby room

Each time a member of staff spends a minute or two in face-to-face language work with children they can put the star or tick up to ensure that for each and every child they have at least five minutes face-to-face language and communication interaction *every* day. Parents and carers at home can support this by adding their language minute stars.

Child's name:				Date:	
One language minute face-to-face	One language minute face-to-face	One language minute face-to-face	One language minute face-to-face	One language minute face-to-face	'I've had five language minute stars today.'
☆	☆	☆	☆	☆	

Ideas for recording content

It is very important to keep a record of the naming vocabulary the child has been working with so that you will know which words they are secure with and which items they are more likely to be ready to give you on request. Also it is helpful to the child to record progress in the stages of understanding words. Record sheets are important to show parents and new staff and when a child moves to a new setting and then to school. Vocabulary record sheets are enclosed. These include ideas for recording content (p. 26), checking vocabulary items (p. 94) and one to help adults generate ideas at home and in the setting (p. 105). There is also guidance on some of the milestones for development of understanding and expressive ages (p. 28) and guidance on objects to include in the vocabulary and concept baskets for different ages (pp. 54–5 and 75).

A really helpful idea is to put up key words you are working on in the setting so that visiting adults and staff know what words to focus on as well as their other conversations.

This will give extra support to the words and concepts you are working on in the setting. This could include the baby room and areas in the main setting such as play corners, outside areas, cloakroom and where children have their snack.

Categories could include

The snack corner; things we eat and use to eat. This could include concepts such as *more* and *big and little*, *on* and *in*, such as 'Sam's spoon is *on* the table'. There could also be personalised cards for each child to show what key words and concepts they are working on. This could be included in the learning journey for each child.

> It is really important to keep a record of how each child is progressing in their language so that you know what needs to be focused on in order to prepare them for the next stage of preschool experience.

Ideas for recording content		Setting		
Child's name:		Age:		
Language record				
These are words I am learning, and you can help me at home.	*Words I can say:*	*Names of things I can give you if you ask me:*	Date	*Initial of staff member/ family:*
To make up my five daily language minutes, can you do two minutes at home with me please?		*Can I let you know by word, gesture or sign if I am:* thirsty? ☐ hungry? ☐ wanting the toilet? ☐ saying 'thank you'? ☐		

Section 2: Activities to develop language at different ages and stages

The ages we show are guidelines only and are not as important as the sequence in which the child's language and communication develops.

For the very young baby make your games very short and interactive. For the infant under 18 months the focused activity with an adult should be *expected* to last no more than one minute. Anything longer should be led by the child only if they show interest in continuing it. We recommend five of these one-minute mini-language sessions spaced out throughout each day for babies and young toddlers and at least one five-minute session a day for the older toddler. The sessions need to be recorded in some way so that you know how many language minutes each child has had and if they have all had their language minutes and it is perfectly reasonable that two of the language minutes each day should be played and recorded at home by parents.

Some milestones for development of understanding and expressive ages		
Ages	**Understanding and listening**	**Expressive communication**
2 months	• Looks intently at you	• Smiles at someone talking
6–8 months	• Shakes and bangs objects • Responds to their name • Looks for a sound that can't be seen (e.g. behind them)	• Produces coo-ing sounds
9–11 months	• Understands little phrases like 'wave bye-bye' • Intentionally reaches for objects	• Tries to get your attention • Shakes head and waves
1 year	• Uses objects appropriately, e.g. drinks from a cup • Can give simple objects on request	• Babbles • Has at least one word
1½–2 years	• Identifies easy body parts on self, e.g. nose • Understands simple action words, e.g. sleep	• Has a vocabulary of 5–10 words
2–2½ years	• Can show you simple clothes on request	• Beginning to name simple objects on request such as ball, dog, shoe • Words may not be clear but you can tell what word child is attempting • Beginning to put two words together, e.g. 'Car there'
2½–3 years	• Understands sentences of two important words (e.g. point to the dog's nose as compared to the teddy's feet) • Enjoys listening to a short story • Understands simple describing words, e.g. big/little	• Uses three words together including some action words, e.g. 'Daddy sit chair' • Uses pronouns: '*My* foot,' '*Your* hand'
3–3½ years	• Likes to play with other children • Understands little conversations	• Able to be understood by most people using three- or four-word sentences with little words and word endings, e.g. 'I like eating chips'

'Bump' to birth

Hearing words and rhythms

There is growing evidence that reading a favourite book aloud can calm a baby in the womb. I have heard quite a few people say that the story they read to their baby in the womb became the story the child most enjoyed listening to later on. The same can happen with songs and music.

Dr Alfred Tomatis[1] found that a baby in the womb will respond to music by moving or blinking. At five months in the womb the babies in his study responded to small units of sounds (phonemes), but what amazed him was that when babies heard different rhythms and different sounds they responded differently. The babies moved a particular muscle when they heard a particular sound. The more often they heard it, the more that response developed.

Dr Tomatis suggested that exposure to language, music and rhythm before they are born helps the baby's later development in a very powerful way. He also pointed out that it is very important to support the development of every child's active listening skills in order that they can focus on and respond to these songs, beats and rhythms of language around them.

Try stories with a rhythm to the language, such as the Dr Seuss stories.[2] My daughter and grandson loved these stories as children. This can help to develop a sense of the rhythm of language. A sense of the rhythmic nature of spoken language can also help with the skills needed later on for reading.

Music has been shown to have an effect on a baby's activity levels in the womb. Try playing some quiet calming music on a regular basis and then playing it again when the baby is born to see if it still has a calming effect. If so, it may be nice to play this quietly to help to bring about a listening, attentive mood where the child is ready to learn.

Notes

1. Tomatis, in Hannaford, C. (1995) *Smart Moves: Why Learning Is not all in the Head*. Arlington, VA: Great Oceans Publishing.
2. Dr Seuss's books can be ordered through booksellers.

Birth to 3 months

Helping babies to look, listen and make sounds

Development supported in this game

Hearing words and rhythms

From birth, babies seek to look at the world around them so that they can learn all about it. You can help them develop their skills of looking and then looking for longer and longer periods. This builds up their attention skills to use later on. The first instinct for a baby is to look at faces. You can encourage good looking skills through face-to-face positive interaction. The human face is the most interesting object to a young baby when they are newborn but research shows that they will lose that instinct to look for faces if it is not encouraged.

The way you hold a baby makes a difference to the way they can see the world around them. Very young babies see best when objects are 8 to 12 inches (20 to 30 cm) away from them; so it is best if you bring your face close to the very young baby. You can hold the baby in the crook of your arm or against your shoulder or supported facing you or away from you or lifted up or lying down; but they are happiest when they can see your face as well as what is going on around you.

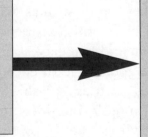

There are key skills related to language that you can help your baby to practise from their first weeks of life.

Looking

Listening

Turn-taking

Sound-making

Communicating

Laughing

How to help

Look at the movements the baby makes. These little movements are the way babies explore and express feelings, and 'talk' to us without words.

Develop the dance of communication. Copy the baby's little playful movements like hand-waving. When the baby pats your face pat your face too, then pat the baby's face gently as a little turn-taking game. Say, in a sing-song way, *James is patting my face, patting my face.* Then pat the baby's face gently saying, in a sing-song way, *I'm patting James's face, patting James face.* Talk in simple words, slowly modelling turn-taking with actions such as *Rita tickled my hand! I tickled Rita's hand.* Change the expression and tone of your voice to keep the baby's interest in looking at you.

Even very young babies will often stick their tongue out if they watch you sticking your tongue out. Try this with the baby but let your friends know what you are doing so that they don't think the baby is being cheeky when the baby does it with them!

Keep your face close to the baby when communicating through play. Exaggerate your facial expressions to make them more noticeable. Smile and make little sounds that interest the baby. Use a sing-song voice and sing simple nursery rhymes and songs. Listen to all the different sounds the baby makes (babbling and cooing). Copy them as clearly as you can in a little sound conversation (but not sad or distressed sounds). Make a sound and then pause for the baby to respond. If they don't, then make the sounds a little longer or a little higher in tone and include them in a short sound rhyme. See if you can model good eye contact. Try to relax, be playful and have fun.

Follow the baby's lead. That is very important as it helps babies to learn how to join in and interact. When the baby makes a sound, copy it and make it a just a little bit longer, or a little higher or lower in tone. Leave spaces for the baby to respond to you. Take turns. If the baby looks at something and reaches for it, look as well and see if it is something that you can move closer so that you can both touch it, and let the baby explore while you give simple words for it.

Looking with you is fun. Babies learn by watching as well as listening and touching. Take your baby outside and hold them so that they can see things moving – trees, birds, washing on the line or children playing, and comment very simply about what you see. This helps babies to realise gradually that the sounds you make and the things that they see are connected in some way. Look at what the baby is looking at and give key words such as 'windy', 'trees', 'children', 'dog', 'clothes'. Babies' brains store up all this experience and language as input that they can use later as their brain and language ability develops.

Bath time can be another good time to encourage communication as fun. Give simple words for noises such as 'splash'. Supervising this at all times, provide sponges and empty, smooth containers to squeeze, drop and explore.

Even everyday routine activities like nappy changing, dressing and feeding can be great opportunities for some face-to-face communication. We have suggested a few but there are many more you can develop yourself.

3 months to 6 months

Some one-to-one activities for developing language and communication

Development supported in this game

Hearing words and rhythms

Dino the dinosaur

Face-to-face focus

Developing looking, listening and anticipation.

Make a 'dinosaur' with your hand by raising your middle finger and using your other four fingers as legs. Gently walk your fingers up the baby's tummy and chest singing and putting the *child's name* in the rhyme. Sing (to the tune of 'Row, Row, Row Your Boat'):

Dino the Dinosaur walking up Jack's tummy
Here is the Dinosaur…

[Pause, then bring your other hand so that baby can see it. After a little pause for anticipation, finish by bringing your other hand down and singing].

…and here comes his mummy.

Each week, use a different action for the dinosaur, such as sitting, running, jumping, crawling. Emphasise the action word by making it a bit louder or higher/lower pitch. Make a spiral of words to help memory. Every four weeks, bring back the first actions, walking, sitting, running, and then introduce one new one. It is too early for the child to understand all those action words, but hearing them often in context in a fun way over time can create an early memory trace that could be helpful when the verbs are introduced more formally later on.

Keeping the beat

Gently hold the baby's hands and rock them gently while you sing the little dinosaur song again.

> When you are confident that a child can support themselves in the bath with your one hand supporting them, you could also use this game using your other hand as a fish in the bath. A little song could be, *Here is a fish coming up to play, down it goes. Gone away*, and then pop it up on top of the water saying, *Here it is!*

Follow the flow

Encourage my sound development. Listen to all the different sounds the baby makes (babbling and cooing). Copy them as clearly as you can (but not sad or distressed sounds). Make sounds and then pause for the baby to respond. If they don't, make the sounds a little longer or include them in a short sound rhyme. Try to be playful and have fun. Smile at the baby in between. If they hold your hand, try some little finger-play activities with songs. Make sure you give the baby lots of relaxed eye contact.

Some one-to-one activities for developing language and communication – Brrrm, brrrm, aeroplane

Development supported in this game

Hearing words and rhythms

Face-to-face focus

Developing looking and listening and anticipation.

Use your hand as an aeroplane. Make some warming-up noises such as 'Brrrm, brrrm'. Then pretend your hand is an aeroplane that flies slowly over the child's head from side to side or over their body from their feet to their head. You could make up a little song to go with it or use your voice going up and down in tone as the aeroplane flies around. Smile and enjoy the game with the child.

To develop anticipation, when the aeroplane has disappeared, wait and say, 'Uh oh, where is it?' and look around. See if the child looks for the aeroplane or for you to do it again. Then start again saying, 'Brrrm. Oh, here it comes', and play the game again.

Follow the flow

When the child makes a happy or contented sound or explores the sounds they can make, play a little game; for example, where you make the sound, stop, look surprised and then make the sound again and smile.

Giving the words

When you hear noises that attract the child's attention during the day, give a simple explanation; for example, if they hear a dog, 'Dog is barking' or 'Children playing' or 'A car' or 'It's raining' or 'Washing machine'. In water play or bathtime, give words for the noises such as 'splash', 'trickle', 'gurgle'. At mealtimes, there are lots of sounds to comment on. When out for a walk, listen and name some of the sounds you can hear.

Activities for words linked to dressing

Development supported in this game

Hearing words and rhythms in context

Face-to-face focus

Make a little language-learning opportunity when changing a nappy or dressing or undressing the child. In order to prepare the child for a change in activity, signal the start of the game the same way each time by saying the same words with a playful gesture and a smile. This could be 'Anne, let's sing'. At times when the baby is sad or upset, this may distract them, or you may decide that it may be best to leave the game for that time.

As you change or dress the child, sing (to the tune of 'Polly Put the Kettle On').

> I'm putting Anne's nappy on,
> I'm putting Anne's nappy on,
> I'm putting Anne's nappy on,
> Nappy on!

Use this with other items of clothing that are used every day such as, trousers, socks, dress, coat, jumper, shoes.

Follow the flow

Provide a small collection of articles of clothing in a shallow basket to give opportunities for the child to take the lead and handle and explore a clean nappy and clothes (possibly with bright colours and different textures), while you name items as the child is exploring them. Make sure buttons and zips are safe and that the clothes have no cords on them.

Giving the words

If you see the child playing with a coat or holding a sock during the day, say, 'Coat' or 'Anne's sock', or comment, 'George's coat on'. Emphasise the words *coat* and *sock*.

Extending this idea to self-care

You can extend the ideas for dressing activities to self-care. You can use these ideas of using the child's name and commenting simply or perhaps putting words into little jingles to use when brushing the child's hair or washing their face, and many other actions.

A little input every day

Developing listening and turning head to locate the source of sound

> **MATERIALS NEEDED**
> * squeaky toy

Development supported in this game

Attending to sounds, track a sound

First use a squeaky toy. Let the child explore the toy by mouthing it, feeling it and looking at it. Then squeeze the toy to make the noise in front of the child. Wait a few seconds then move the toy slowly to the side, nearly out of sight of the child. Then leave a little gap and squeak it again. See if the child turns their head to find the noise. If not, bring the toy  back to the front, then let the child watch as you move it to the side, squeaking it to keep their attention. This may take quite a few tries. If a child does not respond easily to this, keep repeating it in play with different toys and different sounds on a daily basis.

Use your voice, tone and face to express interest and delight when the child looks at the toy or turns their head to the noise.

The final aim is to squeak the toy at the side of the child's head, out of their sight, almost behind them, and they respond immediately by turning their head to look for it.

Development

When the child reaches this stage of efficiency, make softer noises and develop the child's listening for these. Can they hear and respond to a rustling of a newspaper, or scratching on an object beside their head?

If you feel the child is not responding as they should then you could check hearing and vision.

Follow the flow

If a child is making mouth sounds or noises while playing, copy the sound and turn it into a little rhyme.

Giving the words

At times during the day, alert the child to a sound you can hear, Say 'Listen', and put your hand to your ear as a visual gesture. If the child listens, name the source of the sound. For example, 'Bell'. We lived close to a small airport for many years and my grandson picked up the gesture for 'Ssh, listen', and very early on he linked the word 'air-plane' as he was interested in them and had the experience of hearing planes taking off and playing the listening game so often. This supports the idea that children need to hear and see words and gestures linked to actions frequently, and this makes it easier for them to retain and use words.

'Wow! You are still there, that's fun!' Establishing the idea that objects and people can be permanent

> **MATERIALS NEEDED**
> • some cloths, possibly see-through or semi-transparent

Development supported in this game

Supporting interaction

Play lots of peek-a-boo games In the early months

For a younger baby, this is when you hide your face behind a cloth or item of clothing, or even your hands, and then, after a very short while, peep out again with a smile and say 'Peek-a-boo!' in different tones to signal to the baby that it is an enjoyable game. For the younger baby, use see-through material first, such as gauze or voile, so that they get the idea of the game without getting upset at the strangeness of you disappearing. Keep safety in mind and make sure material is not too near the baby's face.

Peek-a-boo games help the child to understand that even when something or someone disappears from sight they can still exist; they are still there. This is an important understanding that develops in the early months ready for the games and activities a few months later.

For the older toddler who is more confident with this idea, you can develop this to peeping round objects further away from them, such as toys, boxes, furniture or doors. Brothers and sisters will love this game and so will the baby if it is played within their comfort level.

6 months to 12 months

Safety advice: There are so many treasures around the home and nursery for the young child to explore, but safety first – always have an adult supervising the play.

Developing looking and listening, understanding, making and using treasure baskets

Development supported in this game

Explorative play with treasure baskets

Let's take the language environment to the child. Between the ages of six months to nine months we suggest that you use traditional treasure-basket work to encourage interest in looking and listening and active exploring. Watching what babies choose to do with the items in the baskets shows you what fasci-
nates them, what they want to test out and how they go about it. Also you can see their developing physical skills such as reaching and co-ordination.

When the baby can sit supported, or lie on their tummy and reach out for objects, then you can collect safe, interesting objects in a basket or shallow container or put the items on the mat and help the baby to explore them. You can observe babies enjoying squeezing, sucking and banging items together to develop their sense of exploration, listening and looking. You can extend babies' actions and demonstrate more actions such as banging, shaking and squeezing different objects to demonstrate co-operative play and turn-taking. There can be different textures, materials that are soft, a wooden spoon that is hard, a colander that is hard and shiny, a brush that is slightly rough or a sponge that is smooth. There can be different sounds: metal spoon and wooden spoon with a colander, boxes of cereal that rattle and beans in a box that sound rather different. Rattles and noise-making toys teach babies about cause and effect. They make great early musical instruments. There can be different colours to stimulate visual interest on cushion-cover feely bags, materials and toys.

For the young child who is not yet independently mobile, this is an ideal way to support learning language through sensory experiences. You can keep separate boxes of items in categories of things found around the home environment such as, self-care, clothing, food and many more. Remember that this activity is always to be done with adult supervision to ensure safe and enjoyable activity sessions. Ensure resources are safe and baby-friendly. Babies and young children will want to put objects into their mouth to explore them.

Let the child play as long as they are interested in the activity. While the child is finding out about the objects in the basket – their texture, feel, shape, appearance, taste, sound and (where appropriate) smell – we can offer our undivided attention and we can, when the child seems interested, link the words we say to the objects as they experience them. This can lead to laying down a powerful experiential language-learning base. You can help by supervising for safety and facilitating so that the child can reach objects and play safely without frustration. Other than that, you can sit back and give your attention as you watch the child explore, play and put ideas into action. Theme baskets can be made up to start with. These are things that we find all around us and items can easily be changed to keep the child's interest fresh.

Self-care materials

toothbrush, safety mirror, flannel, small towel, sponges, plastic bottles, soaps, toothbrush, comb, brush, plastic duck

Things we wear materials

jumpers, dresses, coat, vest, pants, socks, sandals, shoes, boots, hats, gloves of different colours and textures

Things around the house materials

rustly paper, chime balls, cereal packets, small handbags, wooden toy, keys on a ring, old disconnected phone, books, teacloth

Food-related materials

spoons of different sizes, bowl, plastic cups, saucers, plates, plastic containers with lids, saucepans, wooden spoons, colander (plastic and metal)

Things in the environment basket

things that the child is learning about outdoors as well as natural objects indoors

For more information on this powerful but refreshingly simple learning tool, which allows the child to lead the exploration and which is so easy to get together, my early years colleagues suggest that it is useful to look at *People under Three: Young Children in Daycare* (2003) by Sonia Jackson, Ruth Forbes and Elinor Goldschmeid and also *Developing Play for the Under Threes: The Treasure Basket and Heuristic Play* by Anita Hughes.

Learning to look. Where is that Bear?

Development supported in this game

Hearing words

Face-to-face minutes

Make a little game of animating a teddy bear and play with the child. Later, put the bear in another part of the room and carry the child with you looking for the bear.

You can be saying 'Where is Bear? On the chair? No. [shake your head] Where is Bear? In the hall? No.' You can name the places you look including the names of the rooms in the house or setting. You then find him, 'Here is bear!' Give him to the child to hold. Children love playing this game and the adult can make it fun by varying their tone of voice and dramatising it a little.

You can introduce a little beat-keeping into this game by singing or listening to teddy bear-related songs, such as 'The Bear Goes Over the Mountain', and walk along with the child in time to the beat to model beat-keeping.

You could walk around holding the child and step out the words of the songs, slowing down and speeding up in time with the song.

Follow the flow

When the child is exploring and looking for toys, just comment when they find what they seem to be looking for. You could say, 'Thomas, there it is'. Saying the child's name first helps to them to focus on what you are saying if it relates to them.

Giving the words

When you see the child playing with the bear you can say, 'Here is Bear'.

Hearing words for things about me; body parts

Development supported in this game

Hearing words

Face-to-face focus – things about me

Signal the start of the game the same way each time by saying the same words each time, with a playful gesture and a smile. This could be 'Hello, Angie, let's play'. Then, 'Where are your hands?' Make a little game of finding her hands and then sing (to the tune of 'Here We Go Round the Mulberry Bush'):

Here are Angie's hands,
Angie's hands, Angie's hands,
Here are Angie's hands,
Angie's hands.

Over time, introduce other body parts – nose, ears, mouth, face, arms, feet, legs, ears, etc. For example, gently touch the child's nose as you say the word 'nose'.

Here is Angie's nose,
Angie's nose, Angie's nose,
Here is Angie's nose,
Angie's nose.

> Try using the same tune each time for body parts as this may help children to make a connection later on and help when the child is learning to put things in separate categories, such as things about me, things we wear, things we eat, and many others.

Follow the flow

Provide the child with an opportunity to look at themselves in a safe mirror. This can be a small hand-held one or a large wall-mounted one. This helps to establish a sense of identity. As the child touches the face in the mirror, or their own face or nose, say, 'Angie's face' or 'Angie's nose'.

If the child points to you, say, 'Marion's face' or 'Marion's nose' (obviously, use your *own* name).

Giving the words

If you see the child looking at or holding their feet during the session, say, 'Angie's feet'. When putting socks and shoes on just say 'On your feet'.

Don't forget those routine times of the day that give lovely opportunities for face-to-face talk, such as nappy-changing and dressing.

Go with the flow and don't forget to slow your pace of language presentation. You will achieve more if you do.

Hearing words for more things about me

Development supported in this game

Hearing words

Face-to-face focus

Make little language-learning opportunities when the child is ready to play.

Signal the start of the game the same way each time by saying the same words each time, with a playful gesture and a smile. This could be, 'Hello, Claire, Bear is here to play'.

Make a little game of holding a flexible little bear (or toy animal), who pretends to tickle the child's fingers and toes, and then sing (to the tune of 'Here We Go Round the Mulberry Bush'):

> Tickle your fingers, tickle your toes
> Tickle your fingers, tickle your toes
> Tickle your fingers, tickle your toes
> Bear is tickling Claire.

Over time, introduce other body parts – mouth, nose, ears, face, arms, feet, legs.

Follow the flow

Provide the child with an opportunity to look at themselves in a safe mirror. This can be a small hand-held one or a large wall-mounted one. This helps to establish a sense of identity. As the bear touches the child's face in the mirror, or their own face or nose, say, 'Claire's face' or 'Bear's nose'.

If the child points to you, say, 'My face'. If the child points to the bear, say, 'Bear's face'.

Giving the words

If you see the child looking at or holding their feet during the day, say, 'Claire's feet' or 'Your toes' or 'My toes'. This is a gentle introduction, preparing the way for the later pronouns *my*, *yours*, *his*, *hers*.

Slow the pace and enjoy the game

Begin to create finger-puppet characters – developing looking and listening; one-finger puppet

---

MATERIALS NEEDED
- draw a little face on your forefinger or use a smooth glove and child-safe pens

---

Development supported in this game

Attending and tracking

Bring this little 'finger puppet' close to the child and make it bow. When the child is looking at the finger puppet, sing a little rhyme – any song or nursery rhyme you know that is simple and musical.

Hold the finger puppet out for the child to take and explore and then hum or repeat the little rhyme. Model what the game is going to be about by tickling your own face with the puppet, saying 'tickling my face' then 'tickling your fingers'. Gently touch the child's fingers with your finger puppet and say 'Tickle Oscar's fingers'. Play this while the baby shows interest, possibly tickling their face, nose, tummy, and then sing a little goodbye song:

 Bye, bye, finger bob,
Finger bob's going away.

Develop this game to include two puppets to develop looking and listening.

MATERIALS NEEDED
- two finger puppets, either drawn on your finger with child-safe pens or on a little glove, or use one of the wash mitts that are sold for children, which look like a duck, a cat or other animals, or a boy or girl.

When you feel the baby is ready to build on your puppet game, hold up your two puppets with a surprised look and say, 'Oh, Oscar, look. One puppet, and another puppet', looking at each in turn. Sing the little rhyme again holding both puppets where the child can observe them: 'Hello, Oscar, Hello, Oscar, Hello, Oscar, finger bob's come to play'.

Let the baby explore the puppets then play a little game singing, 'Tickle Oscar's fingers'. Gently touch the child's fingers with one finger puppet then the other. Do this slowly so that the child can track the toys with their eyes.

It is always good to establish little familiar routines to let the child know that an activity is about to begin or finish. This helps the baby to feel secure and lowers any anxiety that might arise if they do not know what to expect.

Hold the finger puppets out for the child to take, then repeat the little rhyme. Play this while it holds the child's interest and then sing a little goodbye song:

 Bye bye finger bobs, finger bob's going away.

Slow the pace and enjoy the game

Some key things to ponder on

Where do you need to be so that the child in the pushchair can see the expressions on your face, hear what you say, interact with you and see what you are pointing to as you name something?

When you take your baby or toddler out in the pram or pushchair, try to have them facing you. If the pram is only facing forward and away from you, make opportunities to stop and stand in front of the child to point out interesting things such as dogs, buses or trees. Waiting for a bus is a good opportunity to look around and see what attracts the child's interest and comment on it or draw attention to things you think might interest them.

I saw a young dad on a bus just recently turning his child's pushchair around so that he could bend forward and play little games with his baby son. He was playing peek-a-boo, which the baby loved.

In the car. You can play music, not too loud, when travelling, and sing along to it or hum.

Shopping trolleys have seats that bring the child closer to the adult. They give wonderful opportunities for interaction. In a supermarket you can ponder over the cereals. For example, say to the child, 'Hmm, cornflakes'. Point along the line of packets then choose one saying, 'This one'. [Shake the packet and listen with the child.] 'Lots of cornflakes in this.'

Comment and point to interesting things

If the child is pointing, it might not necessarily be that they want an item but rather that they want to know what it is. Give the name simply, or the colour for the older toddler. Say, for example, 'A red bag'.

A word about dummies and comforters

Most mums at some time have been glad that their baby likes to use a dummy and that it seems to soothe them. There has also been some recent research that shows real benefits to using dummies. But think about when we talk; we would find it very difficult with a dummy or a thumb in our mouths to make our meaning clear. So when it is time for interaction, help the baby or toddler to join in without something in their mouth. Babies need to practise their early sounds through babbling and mouth noises, so make sure they have time to do this essential practice for language.

Distraction

Music is important for children and radio and television can bring so much entertainment and support for learning into the home, especially when children watch with an adult. It is important, though, to remember that young children are learning what it is most important to focus on, and if there is distraction from the TV or loud music when you are working on their language development they may well not be able to focus on what you are saying to them. On the odd occasion this shouldn't be a problem, but if it happens a lot, the child may lose some of their ability to tune into the conversations around them and to concentrate on longer sequences of talk.

At times during the day make sure you have quiet to focus on the language activities with the child.

A very experienced early years adviser once told me that bedtime is a really important time when children consolidate all that they have learned during the day. Children's brains are thought to riffle through their images and thoughts they have experienced and to organise them in their mind. Watching television last thing before going to sleep, she always said, may stop this process as it is too distracting and gives lots of new information for the brain to sort. But a sleepy familiar bedtime story can help. From personal experience, Dr Seuss's *Sleep Time* is a wonderful story for creating quiet, sleepy, bedtimes.

9 months to 18 months

You can teach a person a lesson for a day; but if you can teach him to learn by creating curiosity, he will continue the learning process as long as he lives.

Clay P. Bedford

Naming things with vocabulary treasure baskets

Development supported in this game

Learning the names of things

From around nine months of age, infants become more aware of the actions of other people around them and gradually try to copy them if they are interested in what is going on. We recommend you use the idea of the treasure basket, but now use it differently.

As always, children need to be supervised by an adult. Start off with six items in each session and build on this to provide variety so that children do not become bored with the items. As the child pulls out and explores the objects, the adult simply names them, i.e. 'book', 'sock', 'key', with an interested look and tone of voice.

A list of recommended objects to put in the baskets is included on the next page. Change the baskets regularly but restrict your selection to only these suggested items as these are key naming vocabulary words that the children need to learn, and repetition is very important.

If a child picks up other words, that is a bonus, but for now concentrate on these essential naming words in a play-based way.

We want the children to hear the words repeated many times while they play with the actual objects; that way, both sides of the brain co-ordinate the information and lay down the name with the object. We are aiming at a secure smaller vocabulary. This could mean needing to interact with the object as they hear a word 16 or more times, for the older child who learns language quickly, to comprehend it and more times to be able to say it. Younger children or those who have language vulnerabilities need to hear the words repeated many more times in the games and also in different situations to support recall and understanding.

Vocabulary basket games need to be repeated on a daily basis with the child to help memory and retention. Once they grasp this basic vocabulary, children should find it easier to extend it and build on it later.

The suggested list of items to include in theme vocabulary baskets follows. Use six items at a time to encourage vocabulary development. It is best to mix the items from the different boxes, i.e. to put in the basket for the day a key, a car, an apple, some socks, a ball and a duck. Do this at first, since children might muddle up items from the same category. Later on you can sort them in categories as another learning game, when the child is developmentally ready.

Vocabulary baskets

Language vocabulary baskets	
Everyday items	**Transport**
keys cup hard-page or cloth books bag little handbags ball telephone (old, disabled mobile) watch brush toothbrush teddy dolly clock photo of the child, mum, dad; then later, brothers and sisters and extended family, familiar pets, all laminated to keep them in good condition	car boat bus tractor train plane bike
Things we wear	**Food and drink**
hat shoes slippers socks pants nappy jumper coat dress/skirt trousers	(in safe containers): milk water juice apple biscuit sandwich banana cereal snack treasure basket, including names of food a child brings in. (Include common ethnic foods where appropriate.)

Things from nature * With special care to make sure they are safe to be mouthed by the child	Animals/creatures (leave zoo animals to a later stage)
flower* (plastic) leaf* stone* shell*	bird cat dog fish duck cow chicken rabbit
Furniture	
Real or doll's furniture such as: potty table chair cushion mat television computer toilet bath bed	

Roll the ball

> **MATERIALS NEEDED**
> * soft ball – use a big light ball that will be easy for baby to push

Development supported in this game

Learning about taking turns

Some children will be ready for this at eight months and some will be older than a year before they can roll a ball confidently. This little game will help to interest the child in the process of rolling a ball to other people. It is good for turn-taking, especially as you are showing interest. Use a large soft ball to make it easier at first.

Face-to-face focus

Sit or lie opposite the child on the floor and roll the ball to them. Help them to roll it back to you.

Smile and sing (to the tune of 'Row, Row Row Your Boat') to introduce the game:

> Roll, roll, roll the ball,
> Roll to [NAME] and me,
> Roll the ball, roll the ball,
> Roll to [NAME] and me.

Let the child play with the ball. Stay close and observe what they do. Comment simply, such as, 'Emily, rolled the ball', and smile and praise.

Progression when the child is ready to move on

To develop the hand–eye skills and confidence when playing with the child, roll the ball to them and support them to roll the ball to you. At first this could just be rolling it towards them a few inches.

Later, when the child is ready, move further back to see how far away you can be and still roll the ball to each other.

For the older, more confident child, you could try rolling the ball in different ways, for example with only the right hand, then the left, rolling while crouching down or standing. When the child is much older you could include rolling the ball between legs and backwards.

Follow the flow

Provide a variety of soft balls for the child to experiment with rolling and pushing.

Learning about object permanency

Development supported in this game

Learning to look for objects

Hey, I know it's still there!

Have you noticed that at around eight months, babies will often fuss and cry when their mum tries to leave the room? The psychologist Jean Piaget investigated why babies did this at certain ages and not others. He would show a baby a toy and then place it under a blanket so that it was out of sight. Older babies who had developed a clear understanding that objects don't just disappear would grab at the blanket, trying to uncover the toy, but babies who had not yet understood this got upset  because the toy was gone, and they would not look for it under the blanket even though they had seen it being put there.

Babies develop their skills at different rates and at different times, but around the six- to nine-month mark, they begin to develop the understanding that while they may not be able to see their mum, she still exists. This understanding applies also to their toys and things around them.

The ability to understand that an object or person can still be there even if it is covered is called 'object permanence'. There is no need to teach this ability as most children will develop it, but it will affect your decisions about when you introduce certain games.

We recommended early on in the book that you play lots of peek-a-boo games in the early months. This is when you hide your face behind a cloth or item of clothing etc. and then, after a very short while, peep out again, smile and say 'Peek-a-boo!' in different tones to signal to the baby that it is an enjoyable game. Peek-a-boo games help the child to understand that, even when something or someone disappears from sight they may still be there. We suggested that you move on to peeping out from behind large toys, furniture and doors as the baby grew in confidence. These games can continue and can now include peek-a-boo with favourite toys.

An activity

Let the child explore a toy they show interest in and then slowly cover the toy with a cloth, bit by bit. Slowly lift a corner of the cloth to show a part of the toy then take the cloth off to show all of the toy hidden under it saying in a sing-song tone, 'Peek-a-boo, I see it'. Then put the cloth back. As the child becomes used to this game, if they understand object permanence, they will begin to grab at the cloth themselves. The older child may also begin to try to cover the toy to take a turn.

If the child becomes upset because the toy is gone and does not actively seek it, they may not yet have developed the concept of object permanence. Just play lots of different peek-a-boo games when the child seems calm and interested, maybe holding a toy in front of you so that they can see both you and the toy reappear after a very short time.

Searching for sounds

> **MATERIALS NEEDED**
> - a variety of squeaky toys and items that rattle, like beans in a jar, or clinky keys; one nice cloth then another nice cloth for the second part of the game

Development supported in this game

Learning to look for sounds

Where is that sound?

As babies develop they begin to understand that there is a permanence to objects. If toys disappear they may reappear again. Next comes the realisation that these toys can be searched for. Another step is to search for a toy by the sounds it makes. If the child will actively search for a source of sound when the source has been covered and they cannot see it, then they are ready to play some of these little games. If the child does not search for the object at all, you may want to wait a few weeks before you check again to see if they are ready for this stage. This game can help to develop active listening.

Lay a cloth in front of you and close enough for the child to reach it easily. Show the child a toy that makes a sound. Put the toy under one of the cloths as the child watches, then squeeze or rattle the toy under the cloth. Encourage the child to find it. Help wherever necessary. Praise the child by voice and smiling when they make an attempt to find the toy making the sound.

In their own time, as the child becomes more confident with this game, introduce two cloths and put the squeaky toy under one of them so that the child can see you doing this. Then squeak the toy and help the child to find it. Play this several times in several sessions per week until you feel the child is ready to move on, and reintroduce the game from time to time.

Follow the flow

When a child is playing hiding, say 'Bye' when they hide and 'Hello' when they reappear. Do the same with toys that the child covers or uncovers. Say the words and gesture when a person leaves the nursery or home, saying 'bye-bye' and modelling waving goodbye to show the child you accept this as quite natural. Also model a 'hello' wave when someone comes in or during small-group or snack time in the setting.

Can you copy me? Games to encourage turn-taking

The important thing is not so much that every child should be taught, as that every child should be given the wish to learn.

John Lubbock

Development supported in this game

Encouraging interactive skills

At around 12 months babies begin to copy the actions of the people around them in a more purposeful way. There are lots of little games you can play to develop this interest, but also think about ways that you can introduce turn-taking into these little games. If you introduce a clapping or tapping game or a follow my leader for the older child, show interest in the sounds and actions the child makes, which you could include in the game so that sometimes you follow their lead. This is likely to help the child to respect the initiatives made by others because their own have been valued at appropriate times. Also these active listening and turn-taking skills are needed to form the basis of language acquisition and communication skills.

Physical games

Sitting opposite the baby, start a simple, slow clapping rhythm. Sing a few words slowly in time to the clapping, for example, 'Clap clap, I can clap my hands'. See if they can begin to imitate you. If the baby tries to copy what you are doing and starts to bring their hands together, praise them saying they are clapping with you and sing the song again, swaying a little in time to the tune.

Holding the baby and supporting them with their feet on the ground, just sing 'Stamp, stamp your feet', and stamp your feet, left and right, smiling and making it fun.

Build a little tower of bricks and knock it down. Build it again and let the baby knock it down. This game could last quite a while if the child is interested in it so build up the tower each time for baby to knock it down. This is a great example of collaborative play. Use lots of safe objects as 'bricks', such as sponges, jazzy shiny packets and small cereal boxes. Just say 'Oh down!' when the tower is knocked over.

Sound songs

Make a little sound that you have heard the baby make, such as 'la la la la' and see if they can copy you. You can use this game to develop many of the sounds the baby makes when they are happy and interested.

Musical games

Put on some music and dance with the baby. Each have an instrument, which could be a beater, bells, spoon and board or a spoon and a plastic box or mug. The possibilities are numerous. Make little beating games copying each other. Put on a nursery rhyme tape and beat time as far as possible. Also use your hands to beat time. Sometimes babies can be surprisingly good at this.

Action nursery rhyme games and story reading

Sing rhymes such as 'Round and Round the Garden' or any action rhyme. Read repetitive stories with babies and young children with the visual support of a book that you can both look at and interact with, such as the *The Very Hungry Caterpillar*, which can allow lots of repetitions of words and phrases that can form a background to later vocabulary awareness.

A mother said to me that 'Row, Row, Row, Your Boat' is a great action song for turn-taking, as you don't 'go' anywhere if you don't take turns!

Babies and toddlers will not repeat all your words but the brain can be storing the words and the rhythm of the language for later use. Babies feel secure seeing and hearing familiar things repeatedly.

Gesturing games

Play with words for sizes, such as telling the baby they are '*sooo* big', while stretching your arms right out to tell the baby they are 'getting *soooo* big'. With lots of repetition babies may start showing it to you as well. When you see something of interest, look and point your finger at it and hold that gesture saying, 'Wow, look at that, a dog'. See if baby looks and begins to use the pointing gesture themselves. Keep on using these gestures repeatedly when there is an opportunity. Babies love favourite things to be repeated and repetition is very good for a baby at this age. If a child is pointing to a reference object they may well be ready for the naming vocabulary linked to it.

Puppet games

Use the puppet ideas in this book alongside your imagination and develop little puppet shows where the puppet sings, holds a spoon, bangs on another object in time to a song, sings or dances, runs up your arm and then the baby's arm, or plays hide and seek, disappearing and reappearing, to your surprise. Use two puppets that greet, talk and sing to each other. Use small puppets to begin with and make sure that the baby is happy interacting with it. If not, change your puppet; it may need to be smaller.

Linking to a baby's schemas

Babies explore the world with all their senses. They also develop ideas about how the world works and test out their ideas or schemas about how it all fits together. You will notice that babies and toddlers work through a range of these schemas in their quest to understand their world. One of them is finding out what happens when you let go of an object, and this results in the dropping and then throwing schemas, where infants will drop or throw objects they can reach. They will do this over and over in many ways until they are satisfied that they understand the results. They will then usually move on. This repeated action is giving an idea of the physical properties of objects and the effects of gravity. Little scientists! But it can be wearing if you don't realise what is going on. It is an idea to harness this powerful urge to drop and throw in little games such as dropping a soft toy in your hand or in a basket, throwing the beanbag in the circle or (gently) to a bear.

18 months to 24 months

More things about me; naming body parts

Development supported in this game

Learning and using names of things

Do add your own activities and rhymes from your experience or from activity rhyme books. Another very important area where the child needs to be confident with the names of things is naming body parts.

Sit face-to-face with the child and sing a rhyming jingle involving naming body parts, ensuring lots of repetition such as, 'This is my hair, my hair, my hair. This is my mouth, my mouth, my mouth. Here are my teeth, my teeth, my teeth. These are my toes, my toes, my toes'.

Make sure you choose only three body parts at any one language minute and then repeat so that the child doesn't get confused. Visit the other body parts the next day or week.

Sing (to the tune of 'Here We Go Round the Mulberry Bush'):

> This is the way I touch my nose,
> touch my nose, touch my nose,
> This is the way I touch my nose,
> nose, nose, nose.

Continue with 'pat ears', 'wave hand', 'wiggle fingers', 'pat tummy'.

Try to mention body parts through the day as you put on and take off clothing such as shoes, gloves, boots and so on.

Language is a way of labelling things you already understand.

Colwyn Treverthen

What is missing?

Development supported in this game

Using the names of objects

Have the two items in the basket or on the mat with the child, and after letting the child explore them, ask for the child to give you each item to check that they are secure with the names of the items. Praise the child simply. If they are not secure with the names, choose other items to use to see if the child can identify objects by name. If not, then play more naming games before coming back to this game a week or two later.

Now play a game where the child chooses one item. Encourage them to name it. For example, say 'What is it?' Then put the item to one side. Do this for both items.

Extend this activity into a little Kim's game. Put two items on the mat in clear view of the child. Say the names of the items again, for example 'horse' and 'cup'. Cover the items with a cloth, then gently pull the cloth away, and as you do so, take one item away, hidden in your hand covered by the cloth, so the child cannot see it in your hand. Point to the item left on the mat, look surprised and ask the child, 'What's gone?' The child will take your meaning as much from the context of the game, any signing and your expression and tone of voice.

If the child names the missing item correctly praise them and show them the item. Then remove that item from the little collection and put a new item in. Do this in front of the child so that they can see what you are doing. Now you have two items again. Repeat the activity several times. Play the game several times as long as it holds the child's interest.

When you feel the child is ready, as they can play this and be correct every time, play it with three items.

If the child does not name the missing item correctly, show it to them again and name it for them. Then put it back with the other item. Do not replace it with a new item. Repeat the game by removing a different item in the same way as before (so that it is hidden from the child's view). See if the child can tell you what is missing. In cases where the child is not remembering what the missing item was, try using one item. Then if the child copes well with this, move on to two items.

This activity needs to be revisited regularly on a weekly basis to build up and assess the child's naming vocabulary. Use the checklist available to record and focus on words that the child needs over-learning.

Giving a simple object on request

Development supported in this game

Using names of things

We need to help the child to develop their knowledge of what things in their environment are called. We then need to help them to actively identify them. The next stage is to help the child to be able to answer our simple questions about the things you feel they should know. This also helps us to know whether the child has really understood the naming games we are playing with them and which words we need to continue to work on.

You have now encouraged the child to explore items while you name them, so now the child should be fairly confident in identifying by pointing the basic items you name for them. The way to help the child with the second stage is to encourage them to respond to your request to give the items when you ask for them by name.

When the child has built up the knowledge of the names of items in the early part of this workbook they probably can respond to simple question words, asking them to give you items on request. We recommend that you use the visual support of your social gestures for 'where?'

It is really important as adults that we look at what we say when we ask children questions, if we want them to respond to us.

Blank, Rose and Berlin (1978) said that a child's understanding of questions moves from concrete to abstract. The first level is the 'what' question. For example, 'What is this? It is a chair'. Now we might be surprised to find that when a boy of 7 was asked by his teacher 'Why do we have chairs?' he could not answer her, he looked blank. But when she asked 'What you do with a chair', he could answer 'Sit on it'. The teacher was amazed at the way the simple change from 'why' to 'what' made such a difference. Often, if we simplify our questions, the child will be able to access the meaning of what we are saying. Look at your questions and check that they are at the right level for the child. Any question beginning with the word 'why' is at too high a level for most preschool children to process. Ask, instead, questions beginning with 'what'. For example, 'What did you do'.

In the question games in this book we introduce 'Where is'.

A game to play

Put out three items you feel the child knows the name of, for example a teddy, a doll and a cup. Now put one hand out with palm raised upwards to signal 'Give me'. Smile and say to the child, 'Give me the cup'.

If you ask for the cup and the child gives you a teddy, just say, 'This is a teddy'. Put the teddy down, give the cup to the child and say 'Here's the cup'.

Continue to play the game with the other objects. When the child is secure in identifying an object, replace it with another the next day. But bring known objects back in over the weeks to create a spiral of remembering to check the child still knows them and to support confidence.

Always revisit the names the child is not so confident with and go back to playing with the items in the vocabulary baskets to reinforce the memory of names of objects. It is very important to keep a record of the naming vocabulary the child has been working with so that you will know which items they are more likely to be ready to give you on request.

> Use key words in the wider setting and at home to help the child to remember the names and widen their understanding of their meaning. Remember that these should not be words in isolation but used alongside the actions of things they refer to.

Note

1. Blank, M., Rose, S. and Berlin, L. J. (1978) *The Language of Learning: The Preschool Years.* New York: Grune and Stratton.

Responding to requests for items

> **MATERIALS NEEDED**
>
> - a selection of six items taken from a mixture of the vocabulary baskets, i.e. keys, a ball, a cat, an apple, a coat, a boat, all in a basket

Development supported in this game

Understanding requests

 At around 16 months, when the child has had lots of opportunity for exploration and has experience in naming the objects in the baskets, it is a good time to begin to ask the child to give you items from their basket.

 Play with the child, re-familiarising them with the six items in their basket. Put your hand out and ask the child for an item by using a single word. For example, 'cat' or 'Give me cat'. See if the child can give you the cat toy. If the child cannot give you the toy, just pick it up, show it to the child and say 'Here is cat'. Put it aside and then ask for each toy in the basket, helping the child if they are unsure of the name.

Always work with the developmental level of the child. When you feel the child is ready, ask for each toy, then put it back in the basket or give it to the child to put in the basket. This makes the selection of the named toy you ask for a little bit more complicated for the child as there is more choice involved.

> It is not only what you *teach* but what the child has *learned* and can *use*.

24 months to 36 months

Use the many treasures around the home and nursery to develop a child's understanding of concepts.

Remember your safety checks!

Concept baskets

Development supported in this game

Learning about early concept words

Now that you have been developing the child's naming vocabulary, we provide some ideas for developing important concepts the child will need to understand. Keep the vocabulary baskets and concept baskets completely separate, the only similarity being a basket.

It is not best to cover too many concepts at this age but to reinforce a few key concepts. Opportunities should arise for other concepts to be developed in the other activities you provide in daily experiences.

In terms of concept development, we will be looking at: more, in/on, big/little, on/off.

We should keep the contents of the vocabulary baskets and the concept baskets completely separate. The only similarity being using a basket. At around 18 months, get together objects in the baskets with a view to being able to give *more* of an item. For example, fill a basket with several bricks. Hold back some of the bricks and when the child has explored the bricks in the basket, show them the ones you have and say 'More'. Offer them to the child saying 'More?' As the child becomes used to the game, you can name the toys. For example, 'More bricks?' 'More shells?' Give the child *more* as you say the words.

Face-to-face

Try to use a new concept word once a week and reinforce it in your games on a daily basis. Then as you introduce the next one, use the first less but don't drop it. Keep reintroducing it. This supports the language-learning spiral.

Follow the flow

At the snack table, more drink, more apples. 'More drink?' At the sand tray, offer 'More sand?' At the water tray fill buckets with *more* water.

Giving the words

When you see a child wanting more of an item, say, in simple terms, 'More drink, Fay?'

Parents

Involve parents with focused concept words. Make sure you are giving them only one concept word per week.

Decide if the child is ready to move from one language minute to several language minutes.

Begin to use finger-puppet characters to develop the language of emotion

Development supported in this game

Learning to link words for feelings

Make sure the child likes the puppet as some children do not like to hold puppets. Sometimes, when a child is upset, we can help by showing we understand their feelings even though we can't do anything to change the situation. One child might be crying and angry because they are missing Mum when she is absent from the setting. Being able to say that you can see the child is sad and angry and that you can see that they want Mum right now may help. Then try to lead on to the routine such as using the feelings faces to demonstrate how they feel. This is showing practical empathy.

As a way of developing their understanding when they are experiencing different emotions, say to the child several times a week, 'You are happy', when they are happy. This gives them a word to describe what they are feeling. As they become used to this, you can hold out a smiley puppet and encourage them to hold it while it is on your finger, while you say 'happy'. When you think the child is ready, introduce the word 'sad' when they look sad. Then begin to hold out two puppets to the child, one smiling, one sad. Use the puppet to show what they feel. Repeat the feeling word as they hold the puppet.

It will take some time for the child to really understand the meaning of this activity. You can help by showing how you feel by choosing a puppet face during the day.

Extend this as the child's understanding of the link between the puppet and their own feelings develops. You could link this to a little wall display of feelings faces and pockets to place the faces into.

There is research that suggests that when children can say 'I am cross' or 'I am angry', this begins a neuro-chemical effect that actually calms the part of the brain that is linked to emotion. It appears, then, that teaching children to use words to let us know what they are feeling is a powerful life skill that we can teach them.

Painting positive images with your words

Words have a very powerful effect on the brain and this affects the way we think. We can help children to learn to think about themselves and their actions in positive ways by the words we choose when we talk to them. Once children begin to understand the meaning of words then the words we use to them can affect their attitudes and behaviours, and their self-confidence as learners.

I remember when I was a young teacher in a large Victorian school with long corridors, I was told that if I saw children running I should say, 'Please walk' or 'Remember we walk in the corridors'. When asked now why that was better than saying 'Don't run', I explain that children will usually hear the action word *run* rather than the negative *don't*. As adults we can understand this by an activity I do in my training. It goes like this:

We have finished talking about rabbits. We are going to be thinking about flowers. So do not think about white rabbits on a black background. I repeat, please do *not* think of those white rabbits.

People start to laugh and I say, 'You are thinking of white rabbits on a black background, aren't you', and then I laugh with them because I know, of course, that they are thinking of white rabbits outlined against a black background instead of the flowers I said I wanted to focus the lesson on. We all laugh at that point but it does show that it is human nature to focus on a strong visual image created by our words.

I then say that the best way to stop people thinking about these rabbits is not to bring them to mind in the first place. Talk about yellow daffodils on a blue background from the beginning.

So when a child is running, I don't focus on that but on what I want to see them doing and so remind them to *walk*.

Another example in the setting, if a child is spilling their drink, is to say 'Keri can you keep it in the cup? rather than 'Mind you don't spill it', or 'Emily can you show us your lovely sitting?' rather than 'Don't get up from the snack table', if a child is restless at social snack time; or 'Andrew, can you use a blue pen to draw?' rather than 'Stop screwing up the paper'. 'Dan, use your spoon', rather than 'Don't use that fork'.

It may not achieve the effect every time, and at times, especially where a child could be hurt, we need to say *stop* very clearly, but if we can use this strategy it does help the child to frame things in a positive light as it is focusing their thoughts on achieving an aim that will be pleasing both for them and the adult. This is a way of supporting a child's self-esteem as a learner, which is important.

Concept treasure baskets, big, little, in, on, on and off

> **MATERIALS NEEDED**
> - shallow basket and items from the list on page 75

Development supported in this game

Learning early concept words, big, little (use ideas
for items from the list on page 75)

At around 20 months of age get together objects in pairs, one *much* bigger than
the other. For example, a teaspoon and a large cooking spoon; a little plastic
flower and a very large one. Put them in the basket. As the child takes out each
object the adult names it with the concept words 'big', for example 'big spoon',
'big flower', and puts them on the floor. When the child brings out a little
spoon the adult says only 'spoon' and lays it beside the big spoon already on
the floor. If the child picks objects up and puts them back in the basket, just
name the objects they have put back in the same way.

When the child has had several weeks of naming experience of big objects,
begin to emphasise the little objects in the same way. So when the child brings
out a little spoon, say 'Oh, little spoon', and when they bring out a big spoon
just say 'spoon'. If the child picks objects up and puts them back in the basket,
just name the objects they have put back in the same way. It is important to
ensure continuity for the child at this stage by always using the word 'little' as
the opposite of 'big'. Once they understand the concept they will be more able
to understand that the concept can be described by other words as well.

In and on

Include some containers and one animal. When the child puts the animal in
the box say 'in' the box, and 'on' when the child takes it out of the container
and puts it on top.

On and off

In a similar way, provide containers and an animal and comment when the
child places it on the container or takes it off. Also comment if it or a container
falls off another.

Follow the flow and giving the words

This is an ideal opportunity to comment on indoor and outdoor activities, the
big or *little* toy, and *in* and *on* toys, and *in* spaces as well as seeing the child
putting thing *in* and *on* and taking *off* containers in the setting.

Don't forget that children will be hearing the words in different contexts. They are used when dressing and undressing when they put their socks *on* or take their coat and boots *off*. This is why it is so important for the child to learn language at the same time as seeing the actions it relates to. This then helps to make the different meanings clearer, for example *on* can be used to describe dressing activities – 'I put my coat on', or it can refer to placement such as 'My coat is on the chair'. Children may develop an understanding of these different meanings from their experience, however, some children may need a little help. This is why we have included games to demonstrate both meanings should you need them.

Suggested items for concept treasure baskets

Suggestions for items to include in language concept baskets to encourage exploratory play and concept development

Language concept baskets *More*	Language concept baskets *Big and little*
several of different types of toy animals e.g. dogs, cats, horses, ducks or sheep. several pieces of material of different textures several bricks several plastic bottles several cooking implements several wooden spoons several plastic cups several sponges	(two items of each, one *much* bigger than the other) two flowers, big and little two animals, big and little two socks, big and little two teddy bears, big and little two cushions, big and little two toothbrushes, big and little two sponges, big and little
In and on	*On and off*
Containers of different sizes and one animal	A different set of containers and the animal

Developing active listening

Development supported in this game

Developing listening skills and attention to language

Don't forget to use simple gestures and signs to help understanding. You will be seeing whether the child can identify two different sounds so will be using objects that make a sound.

Choose one of the pairs of items such as a squeaky toy. Put one squeaky in front of the child and the other in front of you. Make a noise with yours, then see if the child will make a noise with theirs. Do this several times. A little song or made-up jingle might help to encourage the child to join in.

Then put your squeaky into the box, put the box in front of you and say or sign 'listen', and then, using a little jingle sing, 'Can we find the same noise? Can we find the same noise? Can we find the same noise? Oh let's see'.

Demonstrate first so that they understand the idea of the game. Squeak the toy in the box and then squeak the child's toy and say/sign 'same'.

Give the child a turn of squeaking their toy as you squeak your toy in the box.

Then put those toys away and choose another pair of toys that make a noise. Put yours in the box and the other in front of the child. Repeat the game to show that the noise is the same. The aim is for the child to identify the toy in your box, which they cannot see, by the sound it is making and then to make the connection with *their* toy.

When you feel the child is ready for this, introduce two pairs of items. Two go into your box and two are put in front of the child. The child has to pick up the one that makes the same noise as the one you are shaking or squeezing in the box. If the child can pick up the same toy with confidence, move on to *three* items.

Developing turn-taking and use of pronouns 'my' and 'your'

Development supported in this game

Understanding and using language

Turn-taking

Sitting opposite the child on the floor, play a variation of head, shoulders, knees, and toes with a little rhyme using 'My eyes, your eyes', 'My toes, your toes', 'My hair, your hair', 'My shoes, your shoes'. This will encourage the use of words related to body parts and also the use of early pronouns *my, your*.

Activity rhymes

Use 'Row, Row, Row Your Boat' as this game is fun but can only work if both take turns.

Roll the ball

Sit opposite the child and roll a ball to him/her saying 'My turn, your turn'.

Follow the flow

Use opportunities in everyday situations to point out 'my coat, your coat; my shoes, your shoes; my cup, your cup, 'my biscuit', 'your biscuit', 'my apple', 'your banana', so pointing to differences in the items you have.

Encourage the child to *use* the words *my* and *your* in the rhymes and activities.

Developing turn-taking and use of pronouns 'his' and 'her'

Face-to-face minutes

Make little language-learning opportunities when the child is ready to play. Signal the start of the game the same way each time by saying the same words each time, with a playful gesture and a smile. This could be 'Hello Angela, bear is here to play'.

Make a little game of holding a little bear (or toy animal) who pretends to tickle the child's fingers and toes and then sing, to the tune of 'Here We Go Round the Mulberry Bush'.

> Tickle his fingers,
> Tickle his toes.
> Tickle his fingers,
> Tickle his toes.
> Tickle his fingers,
> Tickle his toes,
> Which will we tickle?

Then play the game with the bear being tickled. Say 'Let's tickle bear's fingers. Then his toes'. Then sing the song.

Let the child decide. Give the words 'Angela tickled bear's fingers (or toes)'. Over time, introduce other body parts: nose, ears, mouth, face, arms, feet, legs, tummy.

At a later point a little girl teddy bear can be introduced if the child is secure with the pronoun *his*. The game can then introduce *her* and reintroduce *his* until they can both be used in the same session without causing confusion.

Follow the flow

Provide the child with an opportunity to look at themselves and the bear in a mirror. This can be a small hand-held one or a large wall-mounted one. This helps to establish a sense of identity. As the child touches their face in the mirror or the bear's face, say 'David, your face' or 'Bear's face, see his face'. If the child points to you, say 'Marion's face, my face'.

Action words

> **MATERIALS NEEDED**
> * For the younger child you will not need any resources. For the older child who is confident in doing the named activities, you will need a teddy sleeping, for example on a cushion or a chair.

Development supported in this game

Hearing and understanding action words

Poppy's sitting

Begin with you singing (to the tune of 'Frere Jacques') while the child does the activities:

🎼 Poppy's sitting,
Poppy's sitting on the chair, on the chair.
Poppy jump up now!

As the child becomes used to the game, encourage them to sing as many of the words as they can. Then begin to introduce a new action in each session such as walking, sitting, running. Bring back each one every few weeks to make sure that they are being reinforced.

Follow the flow

Comment in simple terms when you see the actions in the setting or in outdoor play: 'George is jumping', 'Salwa's sitting', 'Bernadine is sleeping', 'Brian is running', 'Celestine's cycling', 'Ellisa's cooking', 'Damian is running', 'Holly is eating'.

When the child has played this themselves once or twice and is developmentally ready, draw attention to teddy in a session. Teddy is sleeping so sing a little jingle to the tune of 'Frere a Jacques'.

🎼 Teddy's sleeping, Teddy's sleeping, on the chair, on the chair,
Shall we wake him up now?
Shall we wake him up now?
Sit up bear, sit up bear.

If you like this game you can repeat it in this and other sessions using action words like *walking, crawling, jumping, sitting, drinking*, but always re-introducing the words so that they don't get forgotten.

When the child is ready, ask them during the activity, 'What is Teddy doing? What is Poppy doing?' If the child cannot give the answer, give them the words. For example, 'Teddy is sleeping', 'Poppy is sitting'.

Musical words and numbers, ideas you can build on

> **MATERIALS NEEDED**
> - for the sheep – 8 pieces of cloth, felt, cardboard or carpet tiles, bag with cotton wool
> - for Humpty Dumpty – soft toy, 6 cloth squares or tiles and a box
> - for numbers – 5 pieces of cloth or tiles, 5 large cut-out or decorated fish for the child to hold

Development supported in this game

Linking rhythm to language and words as separate units

With the child sing 'Baa baa baa sheep, have you any wool?' This line is eight words long so we represent each word with a tile and have eight tiles. With the child, step on each tile as you say each word from the first line. Make sure you only say one word on each tile and pause in between. This is a fun way to develop the understanding that each word is a separate unit.

Play the game several times becoming a little quicker stepping on to the next tile at the child's pace as they get the idea of the game.

When the child has played this over several sessions show a bag of cotton wool at the end of the rhyme so that when you have sung the rhyme you can say 'Yes I have some wool'.

As the child's confidence grows you can introduce other nursery rhymes and step on each tile for each word. Play little fun games such as stopping on a tile and pretending to try to remember the word before you walk on to the next tile, and see if the child can provide the word for you. If not, just say after a pause, 'Oh yes...' and carry on.

This is an important game for the child to experience as later it can make it easier to understand that each word we say is separate from the others and this helps to understand reading a written word later on.

Humpty Dumpty

Lay out six tiles in a row for each word in the first two lines of the nursery rhyme. Put a box at the start. With the child put the toy to represent Humpty on the box. Then walk along the tiles, one tile for each word, as you say the words 'Humpty Dumpty sat *on* a wall'. Then walk back along the tiles and let the child push the toy off the wall, and say 'Humpty Dumpty had a great fall!' Look surprised and say something like, 'Oh, look, he fell *off*! He fell *down*'.

Number game 5

Lay out five tiles in a row with some cut-out fish shapes at the end of the row. Walk along the tiles saying each word as you step on a tile: 'One, two, three, four, five'. Stop and say, 'I caught a fish!' or 'Barry caught a fish!'

Give the child the fish. Ask 'Again?' and play it up to four more times. At the end, just count out loud the fish the child has collected.

Turn-taking and active listening

MATERIALS NEEDED

- windmill

Development supported in this game

Developing active listening, looking and turn-taking vocabulary, look, blow, round, listening, focusing and developing mouth muscles

Introduce the session with the little Hello song you use in your setting or perhaps:

Hello [name],
We're here to play. Hello [name],
Let's play today.

Then blow the windmill. You can sing (to the tune of 'The Wheels on the Bus'):

The windmill goes round and round,
Round and round,
Round and round,
The windmill goes round and round,
When I blow.

Blow again. Demonstrate with your finger the 'round' action of the turning windmill. Model blowing the windmill, then say 'Your turn' and pass it to the child.

Take as many turns as you wish within the five minutes while the child is interested in the game. Try not to add additional language so that the child can focus on the key words *your turn*, *my turn* and *round*.

Create a calm atmosphere

Listening to two pieces of important information

MATERIALS NEEDED

- teddy, cat

Face-to-face five minutes

Introduce the session with a little Hello song. Use your favourite or try this one. Say the child's name and smile and sing:

> Hello, Alice, we're here to play.
> Hello, Alice, come and play.

Show the child the cat and the teddy. Say 'Show me Teddy's eyes'. If the child points to something else, just point and say, 'Here are Teddy's eyes'. 'Show me cat's nose'. And so on, asking the child to show you parts of the cat and teddy. Sing a little rhyme or jingle as the child touches or points to the correct part, such as:

> Cat's nose,
> Cat's nose,
> Teddy's feet,
> Teddy's feet.

This is an important activity and should be played in many different ways. The child has to listen to both pieces of information to achieve this.

Sometimes a child can show you teddy's nose when there is only the teddy there, but to be able to do this with a choice of cat or teddy, the child is having to master two pieces of information.

Also make a little game afterwards of asking the child to show you their ears, eyes, feet and so on. See if the older child can give you the name if you point to their feet or ears.

Slow your pace

Materials and ideas that can be used for sessions using the word 'on'

MATERIALS NEEDED

- things to stand, sit, jump or walk on such as nicely coloured squares of material, coloured paper, bubble-wrap, felt, large box lid, head scarf

Development supported in this game

Understanding concept words, active listening, looking, turn-taking vocabulary, on

Face-to-face five minutes

Introduce the session with a little Hello song. Use your favourite or try this one. Say the child's name and smile and sing:

   Hello, Alice, we're here to play.
Hello, Alice, come and play

Take the child to stand on the material you have chosen. Draw attention to the child standing on the mat or cloth and say, 'Look! Alice is *on* the mat!' Emphasise the word *on*. Sing a little jingle quite slowly making each word clear and emphasise the word *on* each time you sing it (tune: 'Here We Go Round the Mulberry Bush'):

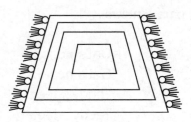

Alice is standing on the mat, on the mat, on the mat.
Alice is standing on the mat,
Alice is on the mat.

Sing this several times in the first session. You can take turns and sing your name into the song and then sing 'We are standing on the mat'. Have fun with this game.

After the first sessions add jumping on the mat with actions and taking turns. Then after three more sessions use sitting on the mat, then after another two sessions, use lying on the mat. Bring in action words you have already used to reinforce them in a spiral of using them in action.

This is a good opportunity to support with signing and gesture

Signing slows down the pace

Follow the flow

If the child shows they want to choose sitting or lying or jumping, just sing the jingle putting their actions into words but always emphasising the word *on* by tone, facial expression and sign or gesture. You can carry this on in other situations if the child shows they want to play this. When the child is confident with the game, provide several types of materials in a container so that they can choose which to play *on*. If the child sits on your knee you can sing the little jingle again using the word *on*.

Giving the words

Look for opportunities inside or outside when the child is getting on or sitting on something and give the words simply using their name. An example might be 'Alice on the slide' or 'Alice on the chair'.

Watch out for the child using the word *on* with meaning in the setting. Use the record sheet to record the words each child is using.

Materials and ideas that can be used for sessions using the word 'on' for dressing

> **MATERIALS NEEDED**
> * things to wear such as hats, shoes, gloves, mittens, trousers, tops, coat, jacket, cardigan, cloak

Development supported in this game

Understanding and using concept words, active listening, looking, turn-taking vocabulary, on

In this session we will be using the concept *on* in dressing activities.

Face-to-face five minutes

Introduce the session with a little Hello song. Use your favourite or try this one smile and sing:

 Hello, Sanjit, we're here to play.
Hello, Sanjit, come and play.

Choose two items of clothing each session. Draw attention to the clothing items you have chosen. Begin with a hat and say, for example, 'Look! A hat! Let's put it on.' Emphasise the word *on*. Sing a little jingle quite slowly making each word clear and emphasise the word *on* each time you sing it (tune: 'Here We Go Round the Mulberry Bush'):

 I put on the hat, put it on, put it on.
I put on the hat, put it on.

Offer the child a turn and sing again:

 Sanjit put on the hat, put it on, put it on.
Sanjit put on the hat, Sanjit put it on.

Sing this several times in the first session, taking turns. Then take turns with the next item, which might be any article of clothing. After two sessions change one of the items. Then after two more sessions change one more and so on. Keep revisiting previous items.

This is a good opportunity to support with signing and gesture

Now is perhaps the time to help the child act out the concept with a little bear. Use similar materials. Some can be teddy-size but some can be bigger and it can be an opportunity to laugh and see the funny side of bear being swamped by a big hat!

A teddy

Use a flexible little bear that you can animate a little by turning him to look around and raise arms. We use a teddy because it is keeping the language content simple without introducing a new name while we work on the new concept of *on* for dressing.

Face-to-face five minutes

Introduce the session with a little Hello song. Use your favourite or try this one. Say the child's name, smile and sing:

Hello, Eddie, we're here to play.
Hello, Eddie, come and play.

Have a hat ready beside you. Play a little game with the child of putting the hat on your-selves. Then, using a gesture, draw attention to the teddy bear saying 'Teddy'. As the child holds the teddy say, 'Teddy put his hat *on*', and put the hat on him or let the child do this.

This is a good opportunity to support with signing and gesture

Draw attention to the bear and say, 'Eddie look! Teddy put his hat *on*!' Emphasise the word *on*. Sing a little jingle quite slowly, making each word clear and emphasise the word *on* each time you sing it (tune: 'Here We Go Round the Mulberry Bush').

Teddy put a hat on, a hat on, a hat on.
Teddy put a hat on.
Teddy put a hat on.

Sing this several times in the first session. You can take turns and put the child's name in if they take a turn of putting on the hat, or your name if you take a turn. If you both join in, sing 'We put on a hat'. Have fun with this game.

Follow the flow

If the child shows that they want to choose one of the items, just sing the jingle putting their actions into words but always emphasising the word *on* by tone, facial expression, sign or gesture. You can carry this on in other situations if the child shows they want to play this. When the child is confident with the game, provide several types of clothing items in a container so that they can choose which to put on.

Giving the words

Look for opportunities inside or outside when the child is putting on their coat or boots to go outside at outdoor play or home time, and give the words simply using their name. An example might be 'Sanjit put boots on her feet' or 'Sanjit put her coat on'. You can also comment when you put your coat or gloves on. This is a good way to check to see if children know the names of the different articles of clothing. Look for opportunities inside and outside, when the child is playing in the dressing-up corner, to comment when they are putting on items of clothing or a painting apron, and when they are putting them on a doll or a bear, or helping another child to put shoes on.

Progressing to group work

By the age of 3, children *may* be emotionally and developmentally ready to do some of the activities in little groups of two or three. An idea might be to offer a box holding an article of clothing to each child in turn and asking them to choose something. See if they can name it. At the end of the game reverse the process and ask the children to put the clothes back in the box. You can do this several ways, for example by asking each child by name, or asking for clothes. 'I want a hat. Thank you. Now I want a sock' and so on. You can also begin to ponder as if you don't know the answer – 'Hmm, who chose the hat?' And see if children can answer you. If not, give time then say you have remembered what it is Heidi!

Keep
your talk
simple and
uncluttered

Bricks *on*

> **MATERIALS NEEDED**
> - wooden bricks of one colour for the early game; any safe materials that can be used to make a tower of objects for the later stage

Development supported in this game

Developing turn-taking and understanding of the concept word 'on', supporting expression, manipulation skills, my turn, your turn; vocabulary, on

Introduce the session with a little Hello song, either one you use in your nursery or the following. Smile and sing:

> I was walking along and who did I see?
> I saw George.
> Come and play with me.

Select two bricks for the first level. Give some time for the child to explore one of the bricks. Encourage them to put it on the floor. Place your brick on top of theirs saying 'on' as you do so. Then hold the two bricks and demonstrate putting one brick on top of the other brick. Put one brick back on the floor and hand the other to the child. Say 'on?' and encourage them to place their brick on the other or help them to do this. For younger children, model it for them and say 'on'. Take turns doing this.

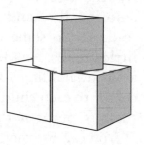

You can create a very simple little jingle to go with this such as:

> On, on, on,
> Brick goes on.

(Take care to say the words with a pause in between so that the repeated key concept word 'on' does not sound like 'non' to the child.) If you feel the child is ready, encourage them to use the word 'on' as they put the brick *on*. Praise their effort. Say 'Again?' Take turns again. The next time, let the child put the brick *on* with your help.

Take as many turns as you wish while the child is interested in the game. Try not to add additional language so that the child can focus on the key words.

Progression

When the child has played this for a few sessions, gradually introduce more of the bricks. After 'on' has been introduced, monitor how well the child uses and understands these words in the sessions and in the nursery. Strengthen by repeating aspects of this game or through other activities that reinforce the concept before moving to the concepts *off* and *down*.

Follow the flow

If your five-minute input is observed by a parent (or carer, key worker or nursery assistant), the parent (or other adult) follows this up by using the skills and key words in free play in the nursery for ten minutes. This could be the child on a toy or putting things on another surface, on a bike outdoors or on the slide, a cup on a table, and many examples like this. If possible, do another five-minute input with the original game or the progression if the child is ready to move on a little. Parents are encouraged to model the concept at home.

Progressing to group work

By the age of 3, children *may* be emotionally and developmentally ready to do some of the activities in little groups. An idea might be to offer a box lid holding six bricks of the same colour to each child in turn and asking them to put it *on* the brick tower.

> Each child reaches readiness for group work at different times

You can use many different objects to play this game, such as large buttons, soft dish scourers, small boxes and many others, and if the child is showing understanding of the concept *on*, you could begin to add more colours and shapes as these should not distract the child from the concept word you are teaching them.

> Enjoy the games and the children will too

Materials and ideas that can be used for sessions using the word 'off' in activities

MATERIALS NEEDED

- things to jump on and off such as coloured cloths, rug, sponge squares, bubble-wrap, solid box lids, carpet tile squares

Development supported in this game

Understanding of concept words, expression of *on* and *off*, active listening, looking, turn-taking vocabulary, off

In this session and for the next few sessions we will be following the child's lead and naming the concepts they are actively engaging in. Another series of linked sessions will follow and in those we will develop the concept by helping the child to use the concept word in a game with a teddy.

Face-to-face five minutes

Introduce the session with a little Hello song. Use your favourite or try this one. Say the child's name, smile and sing:

Hello, Jacob, we're here to play.
Hello, Jacob, come and play.

Show the child the material you have chosen such as a nice coloured mat. Play a little game helping the child to jump on and off the mat using just the words 'on' and 'off' as you do so. Comment that Jacob is on the mat then has jumped *off* the mat, emphasising the word *off*. Sing a little jingle quite slowly, making each word clear and emphasise the word *on* each time you sing it (tune: 'Here We Go Round the Mulberry Bush').

This is a good opportunity to support with signing and gesture

Jacob jumping off the mat, off the mat, off the mat.
Jacob jumping off the mat, off the mat.

Sing this several times in the first session. You can take turns and sing your name into the song and then hold hands and jump together, singing 'We are jumping off the mat'.

When the child has experience of this session and the previous one you can begin to offer a choice of 'off' or 'on'. See if the child can show understanding of the word then see if they can use the words in that context.

After two sessions, change to walking, then rolling and crawling and other ways you can think of for moving 'off' the mat. Only introduce one new word in a session and keep bringing back ones you have already used. When the child is confident with the game and the concept *on*, provide several types of materials and objects of a safe height so that they can choose which to play with. Begin to support the choice of *off* or *on* and use the words. See if the child can use the words in the context.

Follow the flow

If the child shows they want to choose a way of moving, just sing the jingle putting their actions into words but always emphasising the word *on* by tone, facial expression, sign or gesture. You can carry this on in other situations by commenting when you see the child involved in actions involving the concepts *on* and *off*.

Giving the words

Look for opportunities inside or outside when the child is getting off a chair or a toy, for example, and give the words simply using the child's name first to let them know that you are talking about their actions. An example might be, 'Jacob sliding off the slide' or 'Tim climbing off the chair'.

Keep bringing back earlier games to reinforce them

Action words

For each session have a different item in the box and draw it out with interest in your voice or allow the child to take it out. Always try to involve the child, actively demonstrating the meaning of an action word themselves before using it with the toy.

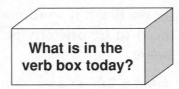

What is in the verb box today?

Early action words to target through the verb-box activity and to reinforce in other activities and through commenting when you see the child involved in an action are: eat, sleep, drink, wave, push, run, walk, sit.

Children learn best by experiencing things themselves. They can then use that knowledge to transfer the experience to something else. For example, 'Leah, it is a car; let's push the car' is direct and the child is involved in the action as you say it. But if you had a gingerbread man puppet you would want the child to demonstrate running themselves before you asked them to make the puppet run.

So in simple terms, you would talk about running – 'Can you run, Louis?' – and demonstrate running. Then if you have a gingerbread man puppet you can sing the 'Run, run as fast as you can, you can't catch me, I'm the gingerbread man'. Then act out running with the puppet using the words you used with the child, 'run, running'. You can also use a doll or a bear for the running.

A bear, gingerbread man or doll can sit, sleep, walk, wave and pretend to eat to show what the action words mean, but always involve the child in doing or imitating the action first, then show the child how to pass on the experience to a bear, doll or gingerbread man.

Follow the flow

Outside in the play area there are many lovely opportunities to comment on the actions of children, climb/climbing, walk/walking, roll/rolling, run/running, push/pushing, pedal/pedalling, and many others. In the setting you have, there is pour/pouring, drinking, eating at snack time, smile/smiling and many others.

Check vocabulary items

Now is a good time to check to see what understanding the child has of the words you have introduced to them thus far. The aim of this record sheet is to capture words understood or used in response to *real* items or miniatures. It is not appropriate to use pictures for language assessment at this stage of development.

| Name .... Date of birth .... Date .... |

Leave blank if word not known or not used. Remember the word does not need to be perfectly pronounced. All speech sounds won't be clear at this stage.

Und = *Child's understanding of words*   *Use* = *Child's use of words*

	Und	Use		Und	Use		Und	Use
Ears			Toothbrush			Mat		
Eyes			Teddy			Television		
Mouth			Dolly			Computer		
Nose			Clock			Toilet		
Teeth			Mummy			Bath		
Hair			Daddy			Bed		
Hands			Car			Milk		
Fingers			Boat			Water		
Toes			Bus			Juice		
Feet			Tractor			Apple		
Tummy			Plane			Biscuit		
Bottom			Bike			Sandwich		
Key			Hat			Banana		
Cup			Shoes			Cereal		
Book			Slippers			Flower		
Bag			Socks			Dog		
Ball			Pants			Fish		
Telephone			Nappy			Duck		
Watch			Jumper			Cow		
Brush			Coat			Chicken		
Cushion			Dress			Rabbit		
Brush			Trousers			More		
Eat			Potty			Big		
Push			Table			Little		
Run			Chair			In		
Wave			Leaf			Sleep		
Please			Stone			Round		
Thank you			Shell			Same		
No			Bird			Stand		
Yes			Cat			Off		
On			Sit			Out		

36 months upwards

Creating a listening corner

Development supported in this game

Building confidence to communicate through talk

The adult could be looking after a teddy bear who has a little bandage on his paw or drawing, colouring, knitting, sewing, doing a simple crossword or sorting a collection of interesting colourful finger puppets – anything you find interesting enough to answer questions about when children ask you.

The staffing of the corner will be dependent on the time the adults have. Fifteen minutes once or twice a week is a good start. Parents and carers could be thinking about doing this at home. The hardest part for the adult can be feeling that it is OK in a busy day to sit like this for a while, but it can really pay dividends if the children see this as an opportunity to engage with you and take the lead in asking you questions about what you are doing. Also, you can be doing a very important task after the session when you record the language of the children who have visited the corner.

The 'rules' for the adult are simple:

- Don't ask the children any questions at all in the listening corner.
- Answer questions the child may have simply and in a relaxed, slow pace.
- Give the children lots of time to think about what they want to say; don't jump in too quickly.
- Listen and give your full attention if they bring something to show you. Name it if the child indicates that they want you to or just look at it with the child or let *them* talk about it; or just look quietly together; let the child take the lead.

When a child comes up to you, just smile at them, then turn your attention back to what you were doing so that they can watch you without any pressure of having to speak or interact, but they know that you are happy that they are there. When the child is ready to ask you a question or to join you, welcome them with a smile and give answers to their questions simply. It might go something like this:

> Tom comes up to watch you. You smile at him. Then after a while he says, *'What bear got?'*
>
> *'Oh he has a plaster here.* [Point to bear's arm] *He hurt his arm. I am trying to make him feel better.'*
>
> Tom might wander away at this point if he has found out what he wanted to know or he might stay and watch or ask you more questions.

This can bring child-initiated talk and conversational skills into play. Having an interested adult who will answer their questions happily but not ask any questions of the child is a good experience. It lets them look, watch, consider and think about what to say without any pressure of time. They can then take time to process and to put their thoughts into words or they might just observe in silence and reflect on what they see quietly.

The most important thing for the adult in the listening corner to remember is the golden rule of allowing the child to ask the questions. Put up a little notice to remind adults in the listening corner that this is a special place for the adult to listen to the child and for the child to ask questions and listen to the answers. You can, of course, reply but not question.

For anxious children, it is supportive to ask parents to fill in a little 'All about me' box with things from home that the child values. Have these boxes in an accessible place so that the child can get theirs out easily. Adults can use this opening to support mediated play and two-way communication.

We all need periods of quiet and calm reflection

Big and little teddy

MATERIALS NEEDED

• two bear hand puppets the same in all but size (you can use two sock puppets)

Development supported in this game

Understanding concept words and names, and supporting expression, choosing and vocabulary, big, little

Focused language session

Draw attention to the two puppets and the different sizes. You can sing (to the tune of 'The Farmer's In His Den'):

Mummy bear is **big**,
Baby bear is **little**,
Mummy bear is **big**,
Baby bear is **little**.

(You can, of course, use Daddy or Granny and other special names if you wish.)

Allow the child to explore the bear puppets with you. Sing the song, encouraging the child to join in where they can. Then hold up your hands with the puppets on and say, using a gesture towards the puppets to draw attention to them, 'Big or little teddy?' Look at each teddy as you say it to give a visual cue.

When the child has chosen, say what they have chosen. Say, for example, 'Big teddy'. See if they can name the teddy and the size themselves.

Help them to put it on their hand and sing (depending on the one chosen):

My bear is big,
My bear is big,
My bear is big,
My bear is big.

or

My bear is little,
My bear is little,
My bear is little,
My bear is little.

Then say, 'My turn [ponder, pointing to each teddy in turn]. Hmmm, big or little?' Choose a puppet. Use the words 'big' or 'little' again when putting the bear puppet on your hand. Sing the song again with the child. If you feel he or she is ready, offer them a choice of *big* or *little* and see if they will choose and use the words 'big' or 'little'. Take as many turns as you wish while the child is interested in the game. Try not to add additional language so that the child can focus on the key words and any praise phrases you give.

After this has been introduced, monitor how well the child responds when you use these words in the sessions and around the nursery setting and at home. Strengthen by repeating aspects of this game or through other activities that reinforce the concept they need. For example, on a walk you can point to a really tall building or large house and say, 'Look, a big house'. Children need a lot of real-life experience in order to really understand concepts, even ones that seem quite obvious to us. But if you think about it we call a toy lion big, but in fact it is really little compared to the family's dog. The big cup is nowhere near as big as the big tower block!

Begin a little group work with two or three children who are emotionally and developmentally ready for working in a small group

Start in the first few sessions by giving the choice of puppet to each child as described above with the song. Then take it back from each child and pass it to the next child. Passing it to each child in turn supports the idea of taking a turn.

Progression

The next step, after a few sessions, would be to pass the puppets to children randomly across the circle to build trust that their turn will come.

When the children are confident with this let them pass it to each other round the circle and model it again yourself when it is passed back to you. At the end of the activity, emphasise the words 'big' and 'little'.

A word about introducing group work

There is a clear developmental stage for moving from child-centred learning to working in groups. Although they may be in a communal setting, babies and children learn language and communication initially on a one-to-one basis and this cannot be rushed. Younger children need to be able to focus on a familiar face and can become anxious if there is too much change. A child may not be ready to learn as part of a group. This is where sequence of language development is more important than age.

Choosing between two objects. Turn-taking, active listening. concept word and verb together

---

MATERIALS NEEDED

- cat and dog toys and a nice little box

Development supported in this game

Naming, understanding and use of a concept word with an action word

Cat and dog toys are chosen as they are likely to be words the child has heard and they will be quite familiar with them.

Introduce the session with a little Hello song, either one you use in your nursery or the following. Smile and sing:

Hello [name], come and play.
Hello [name], we're here to play.

Bring attention to the little box. Let the child explore it then put the box on the floor upside-down. Then name the toys as you pick them up one at a time. Offer them one by one to the child to explore naming them as you do. Put them both on the mat.

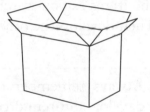

Choose one animal yourself. Model your cat/dog jumping on the box. Use your tone of voice to show excitement and interest. Sing, to the tune of 'Here We Go Gathering Nuts in May':

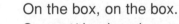
See cat/dog jumping on the box,
On the box, on the box.
See cat/dog jumping on the box,
Cat/dog jumps on the box.

Put your toy down and help the child to choose either the cat or dog to continue the game. See if the child can point to or name the dog or cat before they pick it up. If not, give them the words and say, for example, 'Oscar chose the dog'. Encourage the child to copy your actions with the toy they chose. Over several weeks introduce new actions such as sitting on, climbing on and playing on, but bring back each one in a spiral to ensure that they are reinforced enough times.

Take as many turns as you wish within the five minutes while the child is interested in the game. Emphasise the word 'on' as the key word in this session and try not to add additional language so that the child can focus on the key words and any praise phrases you give.

Parent or other adult involvement

If your five-minute input is observed by a parent (or practitioner), follow this up by using the skills and key words in free play in the nursery for ten minutes. Involve the child in activities such as holding them on and off a chair and commenting as you put toys on a table or on the water tray or outdoors on toys and equipment. Give the words simply for actions such as jumping, climbing, sliding on, playing on.

Take opportunities to give the child choices – for example, 'Richard – bike or car? Barry – skip or jump? Liam – sit on or stand? Sam – play on bikes or on boat?'

Introducing small-group work

If the child is ready to work with two other children you could introduce the dog and three items to jump *on* and invite each child to let the dog jump *on* the items as you watch. Talk about what you see them doing in simple terms. Then develop the other action words as above.

> Always remember to comment on children's own self-initiated play to develop and reinforce their language.

Teddy in and out of a pocket

> **MATERIALS NEEDED**
> - a teddy and a pocket (in a cushion, apron) or little feely bag

Development supported in this game

Naming, understanding and use of a concept word, my turn your turn, vocabulary; in/out

Introduce the session with a little Hello song, either one you use in the setting or this one. Smile and sing:

> Hello, hello we're here to play.
> Hello [name], come and play.

Name teddy, show the pocket or bag and model putting the teddy in the pocket, saying at the same time, 'Teddy in'. Take the teddy out and offer to the child. Give some time for the child to explore the teddy then offer the pocket and say 'In?' Help the child to put the teddy in the pocket. As they do this, say 'in'.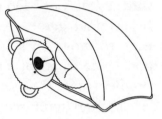

You can sing a little jingle, such as:

> Teddy in,
> Teddy in,
> In he jumps.

Then say, 'My turn please', and model taking the teddy out and putting him back in, saying 'in'.

Say 'Your turn' and give the teddy to the child again.

Take as many turns as you wish in the five minutes while the child is interested in the game. Try not to add additional language so that the child can focus on the key words and any praise you give. See if the child can name the teddy and say 'in' as they do the action.

Progression

To extend understanding of *in*, have a range of containers to hand. Put a bag, cushion cover, brightly patterned sock or glove in the circle, for example, and let children choose where Teddy will jump in.

Model the word with the action again when it is passed back to you at the end of the activity.

In the following sessions, use the game in the same way to practise the concept of *out*, singing:

Teddy out,
Teddy out,
Out he jumps.

See if the child can say the word 'out' as they do the action. If the child shows understanding of the actions of *in* or *out*, then let them choose whether to have Teddy jump in or out.

Parent or other adult involvement

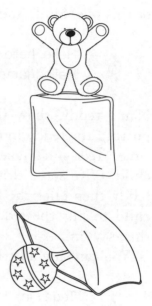

If your five-minute input is observed by a parent or practitioner, follow this up by using the skills and key words in free play in the nursery for ten minutes. Involve the child in activities where you can use the word 'in' or 'out'. Do another five-minute input with the original game or the progression if the child is ready to move on a little. Parents are encouraged to model the concept at home. Always remember to comment on children's own self-initiated play to develop and reinforce their language. This can be at the sand tray – for example, sand *in* the bucket, *out* of the bucket or *in* the tray. There are many other examples you can find over the day. At home, this could be *in* bed, *out* of bed, *in* the bath, *out* of the bath, toys *in* the bath.

Small-group work

This can be developed with two or three children, who are developmentally ready for group work, playing this game with you. Take turns to make Teddy jump in and out of the bag and then introduce one and then two characters, such as a doll and a cat, to extend choice. As the child develops confidence in using the concept, begin to explore whether they can tell you which toy they will choose and what action they will use; for example, 'Teddy jumping'.

Begin to use the concept words together in the setting and see by their actions if each child understands the action related to the word.

> Short, slowly paced activities suit young children's method of learning. Repetition of the word with the action develops language links.

Bricks off and down

MATERIALS NEEDED

- bricks of one colour and shape, initially, so that the concept *off* is the focus and not shape or size. They can be introduced at a later stage.

Development supported in this game

Developing turn-taking, understanding and use of a concept word, manipulation skills, my turn, your turn, vocabulary, off, down

Don't forget to use simple gestures and signs to help understanding. You will have played the earlier game putting bricks *on* a tower. Now work again on the concept *off* and *down* and eventually put them together in a game.

Introduce the session with a little Hello song.

Focused five minutes

Select two bricks for the first level, Give some time for the child to explore one of the bricks. Encourage them to put it on the floor. Place your brick on top of theirs saying 'on' as you do so to link to the previous sessions. Then, while singing a little jingle to signal play, take one brick off the other and say 'off'.

Don't forget to keep bringing your verb box back in for sessions every week

You can create a simple little jingle to go with this such as:

Off, off, off,
Brick falls off.

Pause between words so that 'off, off, off' is clear and does not sound to the child like 'off, fof, fof'.

Say 'off' as the child takes a brick off the pile. Help the child to use their finger and thumb in a pincer grip. Praise for effort. Say 'Again?' Let the child take the brick off with your help if needed. If they just push the tower down, say 'All down.'

Use a little animal or doll to model climbing up the tower you have built and then jumping *off*. Take the bricks off, one by one.

If the child isn't joining in with the action at first, allow them to observe you as you sing the words to your actions. This can allow the child to develop their word bank and comprehension.

Take as many turns as you wish in the five minutes while the child is interested in the game. Try not to add additional language so that the child can focus on the key words and any praise phrases you give. If the child consistently knocks the bricks down, try using other materials such as flat sponges (as always monitor the child's use of them). If the child appears to understand the *on* and *off*, put the two together and sing the jingle with the child as they work with the bricks. Then introduce *down* each time too.

Follow the flow

If your five-minute input is observed by a parent (or practitioner) they can follow this up by using the skills and key words in free play in the nursery for ten minutes. Then go back to the game for a few minutes to reinforce the concept.

Progression

When the child has played this for a few sessions, gradually introduce more of the bricks. You can also begin to use different materials.

Create a calm atmosphere

If they fall over, say 'Down!'

You can use many different objects to play this game, such as large buttons, soft dish scourers, small boxes and many others.

Putting things away together

This can be a game in itself and an opportunity to include language in action.

Small-group work

Language games can be developed from this simple activity with two or three children initially taking turns to build a little tower from bricks that you give them individually. You can observe and comment on what you see them doing, emphasising the key words 'on', 'off' and 'down'. Use a little toy that you can give to the child and ask them to put it on top when the tower is built.

For adults to help to generate ideas at home and in the setting

 At home and in the setting when you observe the children, what words can you think of to describe what they are doing? These could be naming words, concept words or action words.

Outdoors	Large play	In communication-friendly spaces	In the sand tray	In the setting/home

Do you know any signs or gestures that would help the child to understand and remember words?

Same toy

> ## MATERIALS NEEDED
> - two toys exactly the same, a feely bag (this can be a cushion cover or pillow or bag). If the toys are sound-making at this stage it will help to attract the child's attention

Development supported in this game

Demonstrating understanding and supporting expression of a concept, manipulation skills, listening, my turn, your turn, vocabulary, same

Introduce the session with a little Hello song.

With one child

Take one toy out of the feely bag. Name it, e.g. 'Shaker'. Shake the toy to make a sound and model listening, saying 'listen!' Give it to the child and allow plenty of time to explore it.

Take the other identical toy out. Say 'listen!' and shake it to attract the child's attention. Give it to the child. Allow the child to explore both together. Then help them to hold the toys together and look at them. You say 'same'. Use the sign for same as you do so. (Bring your forefingers together for this sign.)

When the child has explored the toys, say 'My turn, thank you', and hold and shake the toys. Hold the toys out in front of you, look at each one and say, 'same'. Say 'Your turn' and give the toys to the child again.

Sing to the tune of 'The Farmer's In His Den':

Same, same, same.
Both the same.
Same same same.
Both the same.

Take as many turns as you wish while the child is interested in the game within the five minutes. Try not to add additional language so that the child can focus on the key words you emphasise and any praise phrases you give.

Parent or other adult involvement

If your five-minute input is observed by a parent or practitioner they can follow this up by using the skills and key words in free play in the nursery for ten minutes. Involve the child in activities such as looking at objects that are the same in the room. Always remember to comment on children's own self-initiated play to develop and reinforce their language. Examples may be *same* sock, shoe, cup, plate, toy and so on. Then do another five-minute input with the original game or the progression if the child is ready to move on a little. Parents are encouraged to model the concept at home.

Progression

In individual or small-group work sessions with two to three children. To extend understanding of *same*, use a range of toys to hand and begin to look at same sounds in the session as well as same to look at. You can use prepared sound-making toys or make simple beating shaking toys. Strengthen the understanding of the concept *same*. Model the words with the action again when the toy is passed back to you at the end of the activity. It is a good opportunity to model saying 'Thank you'.

Putting things away

This can provide good practice in observing words and concepts in action. As the child puts items back into the bag, name the object and the action, so, for example, 'Put the shaker in the bag'.

Use your face and voice to bring out and emphasise meaning. Use simple signing if appropriate.

Same plate

> ## MATERIALS NEEDED
> * two paper party plates exactly the same, a feely bag (this can be a nice cushion cover)

Development supported in this game

Manipulation skills, my turn, your turn, vocabulary, same, look

Introduce the session with a little Hello song, either one you use in your nursery or sing a familiar Hello song.

Focused five minutes

Take one plate out of the feely bag and show interest by saying 'look'. Give it to the child to explore.

Take the other plate out, name it 'plate', then say 'look' and run your finger around the edge of the plate showing interest and then looking at the child to attract attention. Give both the plates to the child. Allow the child to explore both. Then help them to hold the plates together and say 'same'. Use the sign for 'same' as you do so.

When the child has explored the plates, again say 'My turn, thank you' and hold them, showing interest in the plates, not using lots of words. Say 'look'. Hold the plates out in front of you, look at each one and say 'same'. Look from one to the other and repeat 'same'. Use the sign for 'same' if you wish.

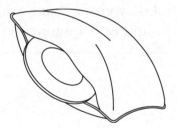

Say 'Your turn' and give the plates to the child again.

Sing, to the tune of 'The Farmer's In His Den':

Same, same, same.
Both the same.
Same, same, same.
Both the same.

> **Children thrive on praise for their efforts**

Take as many turns as you wish in the five minutes while the child is interested in the game. Try not to add additional language so that the child can focus on the key words and any praise phrases you give. At the end you could make a little game, with the child's help, of collecting in or sorting the objects from the bag, commenting on them as you do.

Follow the flow

If your five-minute input is observed by a parent or practitioner who can follow this up by using the skills and key words in free play in the nursery for ten minutes. Encourage the child to notice things are the same. If you think they are ready, see if they can use the word 'same' with meaning. Then do another five-minute input with the original game, or the progression if the child is ready to move on a little. Parents are encouraged to model the concept at home.

Always remember to comment on children's own self-initiated play to develop and reinforce their language.

Progression

After a few sessions, when you feel that the child is understanding the game, bring two more pairs of identical objects and use one pair of each objects.

Not the same toy

MATERIALS NEEDED

- two sound-making toys, a feely bag (this can be a cushion cover or pillowcase or bag)

Development supported in this game

Demonstrating understanding and use of a concept word, listen, my turn, your turn, vocabulary, not the same

You will have played this session with the concept *same* several times. When the child seems ready to move on, play these sessions.

Introduce the session with a little Hello song.

Focused five minutes

As long as the child is familiar with the game in the previous session and has had experience of observing the concept of same, take both previously explored toys out of the feely bag. Shake the toys to make a sound if they have a sound and model listening. Give it to the child and allow plenty of time to explore them again.

Take the other new toy that is different out of the feely bag slowly to attract attention. Hold up the first two toys. Look from one to the other saying 'same'. Then look deliberately from them to the new toy and say, while slowly shaking your head, 'Not the same'. Give the new toy to the child to explore, saying 'Not the same' to the child. Allow the child to explore all three together.

Put one of the pair of toys back in the feely bag and concentrate on exploring the other two and looking at each and saying 'Not the same'.

When the child has explored the toys say 'My turn, thank you' and hold and shake the toys. Hold the toys out in front of you, look at each one, ponder and say 'Not the same'.

It is important to ensure that the child hears the words 'not' and 'same' clearly and as distinct words. If you feel the child is ready, encourage them to see if they can use the words as they see the actions.

Take as many turns as you wish within the five minutes while the child is interested in the game. Try not to add additional language so that the child can focus on the key words you emphasise and any praise phrases you give. Make sure that the concept of the similarity between two objects is introduced several times before moving on to contrast them.

Always remember to comment on children's own self-initiated play to develop and reinforce their language.

A nice small-group work activity

With three children can be to show the children a paper party plate that is different from the three in the feely bag. Pass the feely bag to each child. When they take out a plate, look at yours and theirs and ponder, then say 'Not the same', shaking your head and looking round at the children. Do this for all three plates.

When you play it on the third or fourth session, have one of their plates the same as yours so you are introducing both concept words in the game.

Eventually, when the children are developmentally ready, you could ask them to see if they can find a same or a different plate from yours.

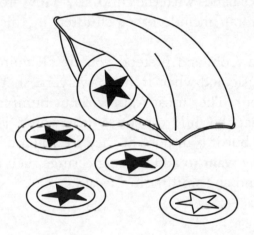

Hello

Development supported in this game

Developing social skills

Pretend you are going for a walk in the park. Play the music and sing a little jingle:

I was walking along and who did I see?
I saw Pamela, say 'Hello' to me.

Say 'Hello' as you shake hands with the child. Say 'How are you?' and smile. You can include other children in this little greeting game.

Find a space in the room and pretend you are all going for a walk in the park. Sing or play music and when it stops everyone should find someone to say 'Hello, how are you?' They must walk without bumping into anyone else. It is not important that the child cannot say the words 'Hello, how are you?' as long as they join in but it is important they see you modelling the phrase in a fun activity. You may want to add other greetings such as shaking hands or waving or lifting a hand and smiling in greeting.

Progression

The children can have fun walking round the room or the outside play area using a variety of steps such as giant strides, marching, tiptoe and so on, but taking care of other people by looking where they are going and walking carefully.

Duck and cat on the box

> **MATERIALS NEEDED**
> - two animals like those from the vocabulary treasure basket of which the child knows the name. We have used a duck and a cat. A small box large enough for the child to put the animals under it.

Development supported in this game

Demonstrating understanding and use of action words and a concept word, choosing between two objects, vocabulary, hiding in, jumping on

Face-to-face language focus

Name the toys 'duck and cat' using a gesture towards them. To make sure the child is secure with the names of the animals before going on to model the concept *on*, say 'Paul, give me the duck', then 'Give me the cat. Thank you'. If the child is unsure, play this asking game until they are more confident.

Then play the jumping-on game with your creature, for example, the duck.

Sing (to the tune of 'Here We Go Gathering Nuts in May'):

> See duck jumping on the box,
> on the box, on the box.
> See duck jumping on the box,
> Duck is jumping on.

Then say 'Paul your turn'. Then hold out both to the child and ask them 'duck?' (look at the duck) or 'cat?' (look at the cat).

When the child has chosen, say what they have chosen. For example, 'cat'. Then play a game with cat jumping on the small box. (He can sometimes fall off and you can look surprised!) Encourage the child to sing 'cat jumping on the box' as you had modelled.

Next put your toy down and encourage the child to put theirs with your toy. Say 'My turn'. Choose a toy, name it and sing the little song. Take turns with the child while they remain interested.

Try not to add additional language so that the child can focus on the key words and any praise phrases you give.

Progression

When the child has played this game for a few sessions, continue to use jumping *on* and then introduce the words jumping *in* in exactly the same way.

Again, wait for a few sessions to pass and if the child is confident with both jumping on and jumping in, begin to bring in the words jumping *on top of* the box.

To extend understanding of *on*, have a range of objects to hand. Put a bag or telephone or mat in the circle, for example, and let children choose which their toy will act on and what action they will use. For example, 'cat jumped on the telephone'. You can extend *in* to including hiding, such as 'the duck is hiding *in* the bag'. Another action word is 'climbing' – 'The duck is climbing in the bag'.

After each session monitor how well the child uses the vocabulary and understands these words in the sessions and in the nursery. Strengthen by repeating the key language aspects of this game through another activity that reinforces the concepts *on*, *in* and *on top*.

Moving towards group work

It is possible to use this little activity with two or three children who are confident with the words and concepts in the game. Start in the first few sessions by giving one toy to each child then sing the little song about the toy jumping on the box. Move on to jumping in the box. When the children are secure with the concepts in the game, you can introduce the element of choice with two animals of which they know the names. Then take it back from each child and pass it to the next child. Passing it to each child in turn supports the idea of taking a turn.

3 ½ years and above – moving on

Nursery Session 1

MATERIALS NEEDED

- ball
- a large, brightly coloured cloth (big enough for the group to sit under). If there are two adults in the group you will need one to lead the children round, so tuck one end of the cloth under books on top of a cupboard and hold the other end to make a bridge
- bear

Please keep language pace **slow** and **simple**. Use 'pondering' to slow your pace and invite shared thought. Praise throughout the session. Say a little about how well children came in and joined you.

Opening round: name game

(Getting to know the group)
(Standing)

Tell the children you need to know their names so you will play a name game. Roll a ball across the circle a few times. Say your name and roll it to a child. Encourage the child to say his or her name and roll the ball to someone else and so on for several minutes until all have had a chance to roll the ball. The aim is to be able to say: 'My name is . . .'

Recap on all the names. Introduce the idea of the group working together for several sessions. Stand in the circle.

Nursery rhyme

(To encourage awareness of rhyming)
(Sitting)

> **use praise phrases**

Hold hands in a circle. Walk round in a circle singing the rhyme together:

> Twinkle, twinkle little Star,
> How I wonder what you are
> Up above the world so high
> Like a diamond in the sky
> Twinkle, twinkle little Star
> How I wonder what you are.

Ponder that some of the words sound the same: high, sky; Star, are.

Sing the rhyme again. Leave out the last word 'are', letting the children sing it. Comment that they remembered/sang the word 'are', the word that sounds like 'Star'. (At this point you are first raising awareness of the way words can rhyme.)

Under

Sit with the children and show them how to make a rainstorm by patting their knees (see **Pitter patter** below). Tell them you are going to make a tent by holding the cloth over their heads (two adults hold the cloth over the children). Ask what the children can see when they are **under** the cloth when they look up. Tell a simple story (waving the cloth) about the wind blowing and the rain falling. Encourage the children to 'Pitter patter'. Then the rain gets softer. The wind goes away and (lift the cloth away) the sun comes out.

Pitter patter

Show the children how to make the sound of rain by patting their hands on their knees. Pat harder as you talk about the rain falling harder, then diminish as the rain stops. Finish by gently rubbing the palms of your hands together to make a 'ssh' sound.

Trains

(Children sit in a circle. Adults stand)

Explain that you are going to be the engine of the train. Go to each child and ask 'Will you join my train?' The child is encouraged to say 'Yes' or 'Yes I will' and they join on behind you. If a child refuses twice use your knowledge of that child to decide whether to pass on again or encourage to join in. When everyone is on the train – chug round – then come to rest in a circle again.

Closing round

(Standing)

Bear hugs: Bear is not very happy. Ask Bear what would make him happy. He whispers to you that he would like a hug. Pass Bear round the group to give him a hug to make him happy.

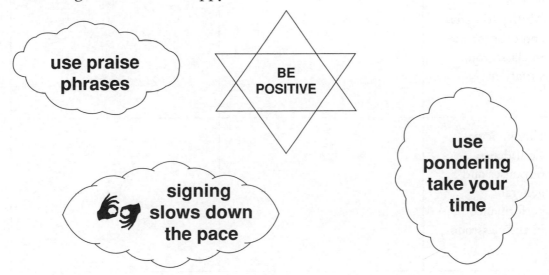

Name .... **Class** ....

Please could you write a brief description about the child's present level of attainment in each of the following skills. You will be asked to repeat this activity in six weeks, therefore it would be helpful if, during the time, you could note any significant developments in any of the following areas and note them down next time. Thank you.

Skill	Present level (1)	Present level (2)
Thinking skills Child's ability to plan own actions		
Language skills How and what language is used		
Social skills Attitude and response towards peers		
Listening skills Ability to listen and concentrate in class/group situations		
Classroom Confidence, responses and general performance in the classroom		

If you have found the previous pages useful and enjoyable, may we suggest Marion and Jackie's series of *Spirals Language* books for older children from four years up to and including eight years of age. The home activity book is a resource much used by preschool settings for super standalone ideas for themselves or to give to parents.

All books are available through our website (www.spiralstraining.co.uk) or from our publishers Taylor and Francis (http://www.taylorandfrancis.com/info/orders) or from Amazon or Waterstone's.

1 *Language Development – Circle time sessions to improve communication skills* (1-84312-156-5)
2 *Language Development Activities for Home* (1-84312-170-0)
3 *Language Development for Maths* (1-84312-171-9)
4 *Language Development Activities for Maths for Home* (1-84312-172-7)
5 *Language Development Activities for Science* (1-84312-173-5)
6 *Language Development Activities for Science for Home* (1-84312-174-3)

Marion and David also run a series of half-day and one-day training courses to equip teachers and practitioners to use the *Spirals* sessions. Individuals can book a place on courses run by ICAN in London or by Marion and David nationally. Courses can be booked by settings and authorities for groups of practitioners. Such courses have been held in various parts of the UK including the following authority-run courses: Plymouth, Kent (Dover, Folkestone, Canterbury, Ashford, Margate), Cardiff, Reading, Swindon, Hillingdon, Lancaster, Oxford, Grantham, Glasgow, Edinburgh, Bridgend. *Spirals* is also successfully used in settings in Northern Ireland, Thailand and the USA.

Note: all attendees on all courses are awarded a certificate of attendance.

Marion also provides highly popular and effective training in using puppets as effective communication partners.

Please email: Spiralstraining@hotmail.com for further information.

Useful resources

(Please email with resources you may have found useful in your setting/country).

An interesting video by Colwyn Trevarthen can be found at: http://www.ltscotland.org.uk/earlyyears/prebirthtothree/nationalguidance/conversations/colwyntrevarthen.asp

Colwyn Trevarthen videos are on language and communication development.

http://www.literacytrust.org.uk/talk_to_your_baby

ICAN (http://www.Ican.co.uk)

Marion and David also run a series of half day and one day training courses to equip practitioners to use the Baby Spirals and 4 to 8 year Spirals sessions to a highly effective level.

Courses can be booked by settings and authorities for groups of practitioners. Such courses have been held in various parts of the UK including the following authority run courses: Plymouth, Kent (Dover, Folkestone, Canterbury, Ashford, and Margate), Cardiff, Reading, Swindon, Hillingdon, Lancaster, Oxford, Grantham, Glasgow, Edinburgh, Bridgend. Spirals is also successfully used in settings in Northern Ireland, Thailand, and the USA.

Note – Attendees on all courses are awarded a certificate of attendance.

Upward Spirals and ***Baby Spirals*** training courses are for those who want to cover the theory and knowledge that leads to more effective practice when using the *Spirals* work in their setting or when supporting other practitioners.

Spirals (Level 1) Training to Facilitate. This is for practitioners already experienced in using the *Spirals* model who want to be able to pass on key information to colleagues in their own setting and to settings more widely within their own locality. This will be an ideal option for authorities who wish to support their teams to build capacity in schools and early years settings in the area of language and communication through consolidating *Spirals* support in their own localities with local staffing.

Engaging children with puppets to develop language, communication and wellbeing. There is a wealth of research in education at the moment that shows high levels of value added for children with language vulnerabilities when puppets are used to support their learning.

Our half-day session attracts excellent feedback and lovely comments such as 'Thank you for a magical afternoon!' 'Interesting and informative session, thank you', 'Should have been a whole day! Thank you!' One-day courses are available now.

Index